The Don Bailey Story

The Don Bailey Story

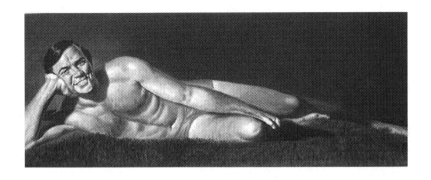

From Truck Driver to Multi-Millionaire

With Jim Martz

Foreword by Don Bailey, Jr.

iUniverse, Inc.
Bloomington

The Don Bailey Story
From Truck Driver to Multi-Millionaire

iUniverse books may be ordered through booksellers or by contacting:

iUniverse
1663 Liberty Drive
Bloomington, IN 47403
www.iuniverse.com
1-800-Authors (1-800-288-4677)

ISBN: 978-1-4697-3458-3 (sc)
ISBN: 978-1-4697-3459-0 (hc)
ISBN: 978-1-4697-3460-6 (ebk)

Printed in the United States of America

iUniverse rev. date: 06/29/2012

CONTENTS

1. The Early Years 1
2. A Conversation With Don And Brother Jimmy 18
3. Birth Of The Billboard 36
4. Flooring Business And Real Estate 41
5. Crazy Stories And Lessons Learned 58
6. Children And Wives 82
7. The Bailey Family 95
    Don Bailey, Jr., and Priscilla Bailey 95
    Robert (Bob) Bailey 111
    Jeannie Sterkacz 114
    Brett Bailey 116
    Donna Bailey 124
8. Friends 134
    Dick Bartlett 134
    Hank Fineberg 138
    Herb Davis 142
    David Rich 143
    Joyce Brodsky 144
    Rita 145
    Audrey 147
    Dick Gonzalez 149
9. Celebrity Friends 153
    Butch Davis 153
    Randy Shannon 154
    Lee Corso 155
    Gary Dunn 156
    Ferdie Pacheco 157
10. Employees 161
    Al Hinson 161
    Debbie Hinson 171
    Richard Faison 176
    Leshan Kelly 178

FOREWORD

I know the secret. And I didn't want to lose the secret.

What I mean by that is, my dad's story from the beginning to where he is really is so much more than just a billboard. What he has accomplished will inspire people and prove the American dream can be a reality.

I don't think people have any idea what he is, the energy he has on this earth, and the amount of people he has affected. And the wisdom he has.

A big part is to have that on paper. There's proof that if you do a lot of certain things, very good things will happen for you. And I knew he would enjoy the book. There is no better topic he'd like to read about than himself.

The climb is what I think is so impressive. And the drive, every second of every day. I think it's a story that should be told. It can help people, change people.

What's it like being the son of Don Bailey? To me, I know the secret. I know the man. People know the story. People know the personality. I know the secret.

I think everybody looks at the billboard and makes their own determination. And people may look at the things he's accomplished and make their own determination, when they have no idea what the real man is about.

He's the guy that isn't just the life of the party, but the guy that makes sure a kid gets a break. Not the guy that is that nut on the billboard, but the guy that bought an underprivileged guy a home. Not the guy that can do whatever he wants to do, but the guy that has helped change people's lives.

He's not just a guy that sells carpet and has a billboard. He's a guy that started a flooring business and a real estate business on borrowed money and is continuing to this day to expand it and groom it and make it better. And I think it was important for me to get it on paper. If it's on paper, that's some proof. And I knew that he'd love it. What the hell. What better present can you give Don Bailey than a book about himself that he helped write? I mean, that's the fun side of it, that he'll have fun with it. He'll make it as big as it can be.

I pounded my wife Priscilla's dad for years about his life. He was an older father, 10 or 15 years older than my dad. When I first started going up to his home, he was a guy that was in World War II and was a fireman, he was from a whole other era. And he and I hit it off, and I'd spend hours with him pumping him on what was it like when he was in the service, what was it like when he was working for the city, what was it like going through boot camp. What was it like being married and having to be away.

I learned so much about him, and Priscilla always said, "I wish I had done a book because it's the only way it can be verbalized. There's nothing else there other than us saying it."

And I wanted proof. I wanted my dad's story on paper, and I wanted it for him. And selfishly I want it for us too. I want to make sure that the story lives on. And it should.

His life, his deal is do it now. There's no tomorrow. He doesn't live tomorrow.

And he's not going to make a decision on somebody until he gets two sides to a story. He'll do it now; he is a follow up freak.

And he will tell you a lead is what you make it. He will tell you that he's been calling people on their birthdays for 55 years, and he's been sending thank you cards to all his customers for his whole life. I don't think anybody realizes, he's the best salesman I've ever seen in my life. And that means being a buyer and a seller, because buying is selling too.

And I've never seen anybody that's a better salesman at any level, or a better buyer at any level in my life. The stuff that he pulls off on a daily basis is second to none. And I don't mean selling in a bad way, I don't mean trickery or deceit. I'm just talking about the selling experience that people get with him. It's amazing what he accomplishes.

He may be the most detailed human being I've met. You sit down with him and there are numbers in front of him, you don't have a chance in his numbers world. He's a numbers man, and people don't know that.

The business side is easy to document with the success. The human side, the feeling for mankind, is what I hope is shared in this book. That's the story.

The energy. The positive energy and the sheer determination to be successful. And fair. Not a bully. Fair.

To this minute he has the will to be great, the will to succeed, the will to take care of his family, the will for others. He's living proof of the verse in the Bible that says, "It's more blessed to give than to receive."

He may not have tithed to a church his whole life, but he's more than tithed to mankind. And it's come back tenfold. Whatever that verse in the Bible is, that he's done. It may not be to Pastor Jones of the church of this. He's tithed to mankind. And he trusts that. He really does. He trusts that if he helps, it's paid him back.

I'm not telling you he's going to get disappointed when people let him down. It breaks his heart. I've seen his heart broken. He will forgive. Won't forget. And I'm not so sure he totally forgives everybody. But I have seen his heart broken many times.

I think that would be a great way to describe him—that he's tithed to mankind. Everybody. If it's the person who's coming to wash his car, or the person that needs a job for an hour. He's going to help them.

And he never stops teaching. Never.

I don't know what he couldn't have been. Does that make sense?

It's not like he's been out-read. You can't sit with him and bring up anything that he doesn't have knowledge of: art, world history, wars, presidents, business. It's endless. But nobody knows.

I think one thing you can say about my mom is that she's the one that taught him to read. Not literally, but the joy of reading. He absorbs book after book after book.

He's traveled the world. I'm talking world history, and I'm talking all of those things that he can sit at a table with and never does. Never does. That's the party of 10 at the table, he will not engage people in a conversation in those terms. He'd rather have the Don Bailey Show, which they'd rather have too. But there's the side that you don't know.

You're not going to sit down and talk to him about what happened in WWII and he's going to know all about it. And you're not going to talk about a president he doesn't know about. And you're not going to talk about world history. He knows it all. And I mean not just a comment, he knows it all. That's why it's so hard to beat him at anything.

He's just not that old Georgia cracker that everybody initially thinks he is. The energy, and I don't mean just getting through the day. There's a spirit.

Irreplaceable. And not comparable. Nobody.

And he knows what he knows. He never says he knows more than that guy in his business world and his life. He's a master of his world. And he'll go anywhere. He's not bashful, not shy, not out of place at this stage of his life. He loves being around athletes, he loves being around coaches. He loves meeting new people.

And he'll be the first to tell you, he'll go on a week's cruise and they leave Saturday, and he wants his ass off that boat Tuesday. Vacation was over Tuesday. Not enough to keep him busy. He needs the rest, but his gasoline is human interaction.

Other than his story becoming a movie—ha, ha—I don't think there's anything that he personally would enjoy more than this book. I thought it would be one of the best gifts that he could ever receive. And I'm sure there's going to be a second edition.

—Don Bailey, Jr.

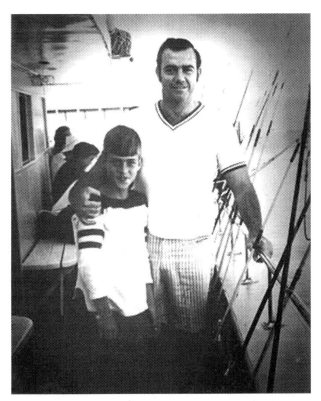

Don on a fishing trip with young Don.

1. THE EARLY YEARS

Dad had just gone bankrupt. Of course you didn't file anything. You had no money and you went out of business. He had a little dry goods store, they called it. Sold clothes and groceries, pickles in a barrel, in Dacula, Georgia., which is about one block long across from a little rail station. We used to take the cotton and sell it and load it on a train and ship it out. Dacula is pretty close to Athens. It's north of Atlanta going towards Athens where Ed Pope (of the Miami Herald) was born. We go back there now every few years for a family reunion.

So he had no job. We were living in a little farm house out in the country, with of course an outside bathroom and no electricity, just kerosene lamps, which was common back in the country there.

His friend Mark Stanley had moved to Miami a couple years before and he wrote my dad right after he went out of business and sent a letter saying he was doing real good in the grocery business and dad ought to come down. He said, "If you come down you're going to stay because you'll get sand in your shoes."

I don't know if you remember that slogan. Years ago they had on the post cards: Come to Florida, Come to Miami, Get sand in your shoes.

Dad went to Florida, I don't know for how long. My brother and I were out there playing in the yard and he drove up and he had a one-seated car, one seat across and a little thing in the back. He got out of the car and said, "I brought you a present." Then he threw a coconut out. Not a green one, one that was kind of brown and dried up. He said, "That milk in there is good, the coconut is good. That's what they eat in Florida, and they drink that juice."

For two days we tried to open it. Finally we threw it into the hog pen. They were bumping it and trying to bite it.

As he got out of the car and threw it to us, he said, "Boys, we're going to Florida, I've got sand in my shoes." I had no clue what he meant.

But soon thereafter we got in the car. It was my older brother Jack, in front with my dad driving and my mother on the other side and Jimmy and I in the crawl space. Me 5 and him 3. There was no expressway to Miami. We came down U.S. 1 all the way. We got somewhere in mid-Florida and there was a smell of sulphur and my brother Jack thought it was me farting back there and he turned around and started hitting me. My dad told him to stop it and told Jack what it was, and Jack didn't believe him because he'd smelled it before. It could have been me but it wasn't.

We came to Miami and he opened a little grocery store. He had $150.

First of all, we stayed with my cousin Dorothy, who lived a block from the old Sears building, which is now the Arscht Center. They still have that one part of the Sears building standing. She and her husband, Arthur Baldwin, who was a pioneer Miamian, had a little old wood house and we slept on what we called pallets. That was just a quilt on the floor. Jim and I slept on the floor.

A few days later he took us to the little grocery store he rented and there was one room in the back, just one small room. This is where our family of five was to live. It had no bathtub, no shower. They had a sink, and my mother would wash my feet, my face and my hands every night. Saturday night they would fill a big metal tub with water and my dad bathed first, my brother Jack second, me third, Jim fourth, my mother fifth. All in the same water, once a week. We lived there probably a couple of years.

Even though $150 then was a lot more than it is today, in his grocery store he had two things of each to sell. Two Spams, two peanut butters, two jellies, two this, two that. I had two older, half brothers, Neil and Gene, who stayed in Georgia. Neil came down and painted the sign

"Gene's Cash Grocery" and hung it above the store's entrance. We were maybe 200 feet, out of what's called Overtown today. The community started coming in and they'd buy. There was one other grocery store around but it was a block past us, so they stopped at the first one. He got a few more cans and over a few years, he had stock in the grocery store and was doing a great business.

My mother and father worked seven days a week. He would get up before daylight and go to the market. It was open air and he'd drive through in an old car that had those big fenders, and he'd buy a 100-pound sack of potatoes, 100 pounds of onions. He would fill the back seat with stuff, and my brother and I would sit in the front seat with him. We didn't go too often because we didn't want to get up that early. Maybe a Saturday or Sunday. And each time he would sing, "This little piggy went to market." I remember being happy every day. I never knew I was poor, because we always got something to eat.

I learned what not to do in real estate from my dad's mistakes. When he was doing well in the original grocery store he bought a house for $800 and sold it for $2,800 in about a month. Then he bought a three-unit apartment house, and a four unit and I think he got them all for around $12,000. Somebody came along and offered him $8,000 for his business. He thought he had enough money to retire for life. He might have been 70 at that time. He made the mistake—he never continued in real estate. He spent the money. He got a taste of it and figured, "I can make money whenever I want to."

He sold the two apartment houses that brought in income to buy a home in a better neighborhood to raise Jim and I. His neighbors were T.V. Moore, the guy that had Moore's Wholesale; Dave who had Dave's Eggs. The other neighbor was Davis, the mother and father who originated Winn-Dixie. That was a real ritzy neighborhood, but all his money was sunk in that house and he had no income. He bought that little grocery store on Miami Avenue and 45th Street and thought he could make it but he didn't.

He started off getting cash for his groceries and then he started giving charge accounts, and people didn't pay him. I remember my mother would take me and Jimmy around and we'd go knock on doors on Sunday morning late. People would say, "What do you want?" It was a rough neighborhood. They would cuss her out, because some would still be sleeping, slam doors. She very seldom got any money.

That's why in my business I told my son and employees we don't give credit. There's a few exceptions, like Holiday Inn and the University of Miami. But we don't give credit because you just don't get paid. Just like Benjamin Franklin said, neither a borrower nor a lender be.

Another lesson that really taught me about giving credit, my second oldest brother came to me one day and he knew that I had $5,000 that I'd saved up, which was a lot of money. My first wife called it the Holy Five because I'd never touch it. During my second marriage, I still didn't touch it. Gene came over and said, "Don can I buy you lunch?" So we walked across the street and he said, "I'm a little tight. I hear you've got $5,000. I need to borrow $2,500. I can pay you back in 90 days and I'll give you interest."

I said, "Gene, you're my brother, I'll be glad to loan it to you and I don't want interest." Sure enough 90 days later he came and said, "Don I want to buy you lunch." We go across the street and I'm ready to count the money. He says, "I need that other $2,500. I can pay it back. It's going to take about six months to pay it back."

I loaned it to him and it took 11 years to get it back. I started to harassing him and going to his house, and he was married to a millionaire's daughter and they had money. But he was a drunk.

He finally paid me back and said, "You notice I put $500 dollars in interest." I said, "I don't want it. I'm not keeping it. I'm not taking it. I'll give it to my dad." So I cashed it and gave it to my dad. And I never liked him again, never. He was the meanest, worst guy. He actually bought a car from my dad and didn't pay him for it. My dad got another small grocery store near Jackson Memorial Hospital but he only had it for about a year and Gene went over to him and said, "Hey, I don't have a job, let me buy this grocery store. I'll pay you every week and give you part of the profits and you'll never have to work."

He never paid him a penny, sold all the inventory out and the grocery store closed. That was Gene, second from the oldest. My other brothers I really love.

Nearly every summer we'd go back to Georgia. They would leave me with my grandmother at first, which is on my mother's side, and Jim with his sister. When I got to be about 10, I stayed with my mom's sister, Aunt Bertie and my Uncle Fonny. It scared me the first time I met Uncle Fonny because he stuck his hand out—because he always wanted to shake your hand but all he had was a little finger and a thumb. All the fingers had been cut off while doing mill work with a saw. So it was like a lobster grabbing you. I think he enjoyed doing this the first time meeting someone before they knew what to expect. Any time he met somebody he'd stick that hand out. He liked the look on their faces. It scared the hell out of me. I didn't know what I got my hand into.

They didn't have kids, and they wanted one. I guess my mom and dad had told them they really couldn't afford to keep all three kids and feed them, so they wanted to adopt me. They had a nice farm with horses and cows. I didn't know about the adoption plans until afterwards. That summer, the first night she brought this big bowl, which I thought was hot soup. And I said, "Is that something to eat?" And she said, "No, if you have to pee you pee in this. If you have to do the other thing, you do that here" and pointed out the window to the outhouse out back. There was no inside bathroom.

They would wake up before sunrise and later they would wake me up. When they woke me up they had already fed the chickens, milked the cows, fed the mules, fed the horses and it was still dark. She would have a dozen eggs cooked every morning, and a batch of biscuits, as she called it. Sliced, smoked, real salty ham where they used to hang a pig and salt cure it in the barn. When you want ham you just go and slice some. Pure salt. I developed a taste for it.

The milk they served was another story. Bitter weed would grow in the fields. They called whole milk sweet milk, which tasted like bitter weed. It was very bitter. You got used to it after awhile. That was the only thing on the table to drink. It didn't bother them, they'd been drinking it for years. I almost got accustomed to that horrid taste.

After the end of that summer, and after spending a summer with me—they decided they didn't want any kids. So they sent me back. That's when my parents told me the plan for adoption. They said they were sorry, they just needed help. I still went back every summer until I was maybe 14 or 15.

I was born in 1933. So the auction of my grandparents' farm must have happened in 1938. I remember my mother's parent's, June Hezekiah and Ila May. They had a farm with a red brick house and I remember the attic. I remember my mother, grandmother and Jim and I were up in the attic and we were looking out the window. My mother and my grandmother were crying because they saw them auction off their things one by one—the wagons, the plows, the mules, the horses, the cows, and all sorts of farming implements.

I can remember my grandmother's comments during this painful event. She said, "I knew Mr. Maynard would be here. He's been wanting these cows for a long time. He loves that horse." And on and on. When she wasn't crying she was criticizing the people who were there buying stuff to pay off their debts. She shouldn't have. I mean, it's an auction. And anybody could buy it. It was just their neighbors. She figured if they didn't buy it maybe they could keep it.

Somehow they kept the farm and they kept a cow. They may not have kept that cow but they got another cow. In later years they'd talk about that big cow and how much milk it gave. They also kept the chickens.

My grandfather taught me how to ring a chicken's neck. I didn't want to do it, and I'm not 10 years old yet. He made me pick up that chicken and start swinging around until it's neck came off. And I took a swing or swing and a half, and I dropped it. I just couldn't do it. And the chicken started running around and my grandfather grabbed it and he finished the job.

He rung a chicken's neck every other day because there was no Winn-Dixie, no Kwik Chek out in the country. He had cantaloupes, watermelon, and a peach grove and an big apple tree.

They lived there for several more years.

My mother, Maitre Bird Bailey, got word somehow that her mother had died. She grabbed Jim and me and jumped into the car to go to Georgia for the funeral. She told us all the time that Raliegh Attriss Bailey, our father, was so smart that he could have been President if he had finished the 9th grade. We were headed north on US 1 and got as far as the circle in Hollywood and she couldn't figure out where U.S. 1 continued. We must have gone around that circle several times before she decided to go back home. She told my dad, "I don't how to get to Georgia on my own." And he said, "I'm glad you came back, it's my mother that died, not your mother."

Dad left us at home and he took off for Georgia.

He got through the circle. Remember, he could have been President.

I was around 10. I would hang around the grocery store, and I asked my mom, "You teach me how to make change." So she worked with me and I got to be the cashier.

After awhile, when business was getting pretty good, I took a $20 bill out and $20 was a lot of money. I went down to Bayfront Park. The Navy fleet was in and it was a big deal. I was at a crowded hot dog stand and paid with my stolen $20. Waiting for my change I spotted my father in the crowd close by. Fortunately he was really drunk and did not see me. This must have been a Sunday, and that's when Dad did his heavy drinking. I was really afraid. If he saw that $20—I don't know what it's worth today, my God, I stood there and got the change and I said, "Oh, boy, I'm never going to steal money out of the cash register again."

But I did. Every now and then I'd take a little bit.

My mother caught me in a lie because on her birthday I gave her a set of dishes and I gave her all kinds of stuff. As a kid you don't connive or think.

And she says, "Where'd you get the money to buy this?"

"Well, Herb Davis or somebody. Raymond Athens' mother didn't need these any more."

She said, "Don, that's not true. Are you stealing money out of the cash register? I know you are, I know you are."

So I admitted it and I was never a cashier again.

In my 20's, when I became manager at Harry Rich Carpets, I caught a guy stealing. I went up to the boss and said, "Here's what he stole, I saw him do it. He admitted it."

He said, "Well I don't blame him. I blame you because you didn't have the guidelines and procedures to keep him from stealing. It was your fault that he stole, not his." He said, "You cannot tempt people and expect them to stay honest." To this day I try and avoid cash transactions—I'll get a cashier's check because I don't want anyone to yield to temptation. That was a good lesson I learned.

When I was in my teens working at Tanner's grocery store as a stock boy and bagging groceries. I worked there after school and on Saturdays I'd take the bus down and be there at 8 and work until 9 at night. Fifty cents an hour, plus tips.

I got my friend a job there, and a few years go by and they made him a cashier. And one night a week the manager and the assistant manager were off, just the cashiers were there. They left somebody in charge but he'd go out for about a three-hour dinner. The cashier that I'd gotten the job, he came up with an idea that all his friends could fill their cart and just give him $10. I would fill my basket up with things to help my father's failing store down the street.

My father had sold the original store that was doing well. He needed time to rest and thought he could open another store later and it would be successful. He spent all the money from the sale and tried to start again and it never worked. During that period—I was at Tanners and would stock his store with items from Tanners . . . because all I remember that he had was a lot of chutney and he didn't know what chutney was and neither did I. It's like mango chutney, like sliced mangos or guava or something. But he had very little stuff, mostly milk and bread and apples and stuff. Jim and I would stock the shelves with the items we got for $10. Mainly we stuck with small items like toothpaste and meat and coffee. Tanners started seeing the inventory disappear, and they got their record of their financial report and they fired a bunch people and I had already quit.

When I was in high school, maybe 10th or 11th grade, I would go to work stocking groceries at night from 11 to 6 in the morning then shower and go to school. I would get out of school at 3 and go home and sleep and then go back to work. The hours took a toll and so did the bus ride over to Collins Ave. Next I worked for a laundry after school.

My job was to sort clothes. I had no clue what clothes went where. I probably ruined more clothes putting blues with whites, whatever.

I remember they made you finish your pile before they let you leave even though it was 12. And the busses stopped running at 12. So if I didn't finish—the laundry was on 10th Street and we lived on 47th Street—I would have to walk home.

But it didn't happen often. I made sure that I got out of there on time.

That was the period that my parents had to rent the house to pay the mortgage. We moved to a one room apartment. My dad slept on one side on a day bed and my mother slept on the other side on a day bed, Jimmy and I slept in the middle of the floor on a pallet. Jack had already married at 16, married a 14-year-old girl. He did not want to marry her, but my mother said you have touched her, you've got to marry her or you'll go to jail. So he married her. They ran away to Georgia and got married.

At night I could hear my parents talking about having no money. "Raliegh, I don't know what I'm going to do, there's no money," he said. "We'll get the rent from the house and that will pay the mortgage, and we've got the grocery store. We can take a little groceries so we won't starve." My older brother, Gene, his son from another marriage, had told him to put a little money into Social Security for a few years. Finally he started to get some Social Security checks and things got a little better because he was retirement age and he had two children at home.

My whole desire when I was in the eighth or ninth grade was to play football. I loved to watch it, I loved to play it. We played sandlot football. We would go over to the graveyard between Miami Avenue and Northeast 2nd Avenue, to a vacant lot next door. Twenty, 30, maybe 40 kids would show up there, barefoot, and play sandlot football. And I loved it.

I was hanging around Joe Brodsky then. Even though I was supposed to go to Edison, he was in the Jackson area. So I went to Jackson and I thought I was pretty good. At that time I was only about 145 pounds. Coach Roy French told me, "You know, Don, I like big guys on the line.

To be honest with you, you can come out and play here but you're not going to be first team ever."

I stayed there in the 10th grade and part of the 11th and then I transferred to Coral Gables. One of my coaches from Jackson called the coach at Coral Gables and said, "This guy's got the desire and is fast." So I went out for spring football and I made first string right away.

That was a long way to travel to school everyday. I went with Calvin Kaye, who later became a dentist. It was so long we decided to skip school a lot, we didn't last there very long. We transferred to Miami Tech. It was closer. I went out for football there and I made first string. I remember the big star there was Maylin Smith. I only stayed at Miami Tech awhile and then I went to Edison and I went out for football. Harvey James, who later became a father figure to me, who I dearly loved, gave me a chance to prove myself. I guess the athletic budget was low, because all they had left to give me was a Jim Thorpe leather helmet and the shoes were so large that they curled up and the pants came down to my ankles. I looked like a clown. He may have done it on purpose. It ticked me off, made me a fighter. I was already ticked off because when I was in the fourth grade I had chipped both teeth and a short time later I lost one of them. So going to new schools with missing front teeth had made me pretty ornery. I remember the first string offensive guards were Hubert Martin and Bob Hipke. Hipke later became a coach at Hialeah. They lined two on one and I went through 'em like they weren't there. They stopped the football practice to see the new guy dressed like Jim Thorpe.

My brother Jimmy was there. He was on the B squad. They stopped their practice to watch me do it over and over again. I was feeling pretty confident, but in the spring game they didn't put me in until the last quarter. I was fuming mad. I played hard. The next morning we're supposed to go to practice and go over the game and I didn't go. I thought to hell with it. Then Coach Harvey James calls me.

"Bailey! Where are you?"

I said, "I'm at home."

"Why aren't you here?"

I said, "I went out there, I practiced all this time, I'm better than anybody and you put me in at the end of the game."

He said, "But you made more tackles in one quarter than the guy before you made in three quarters. You're now the starting nose guard."

Next year we won nine straight games. The 10th game 42,000 showed up at the Orange Bowl in hopes of Edison finally beating Miami High after 40 years of losing to them, but they beat us. We had beaten Jackson that year and Miami lost to Jackson, so our hopes were high. Edison beat them the next year and I was gone. In that last game, I was on fire. My brother will tell you, about every third tackle the announcer would say, "Bailey on the tackle." They didn't do the statistics so much back then but I was in on just about every tackle, because I was fast off the ball, really fast. I used my hands. And most of the defensive players back then, even though it was legal, didn't push them or pull them down. Instead they blocked. Not me. Harvey James stopped practice one day and said, "Why is he the only one using his hands?"

I'd never gotten any attention from any adult because my dad and mom worked all the time. Harvey James gave me a lot of attention, not necessarily complimentary but you knew where his heart was.

I'll never forget the game I was bleeding really bad on my arm. Really bad. When I came out of the game I said, "Coach, coach, look at all this blood." He said, "Rub some dirt in it, Bailey, and get your ass back out there." And I went out there and I never complained again.

Years later, when he found out I was working for Harry Rich Carpets as a salesman, he came in and bought carpet and he sent in all the Edison teachers for their floors. We stayed in contact until the day he died. I gave him a Christmas present every year. Right before he died he came to my store to say hello. What a wonderful guy.

I never studied or did homework the entire 12 years I went to school. I could pretty much pick up everything in class, but where I ran into trouble was in the 11th grade. That was the year I changed school so much, so it was impossible to make sense of any of my classes. But I wanted to play football and you couldn't do it failing classes. Thankfully Coach James went to the teachers and convinced them to give me D's so I could play football. That was a huge favor because it kept me not only in football, but also in school.

I did have a desire to play college football. But when I got out of school and had no money. I worked for Supreme Meats delivering meat and I beefed up to 190 pounds and I saved my money. First got my teeth fixed and thought I'd saved enough money to go to college for four years. So I went to Florida State. All my friends went to Florida. They were mostly wealthier kids, or on scholarship. But I didn't want to be around them, I wanted to devote my time to studying. So I figured I should go to Tallahassee where I didn't know anyone. So I worked about a year, a year and a half, after I got out of school.

My old buddy the cashier from Tanners and I paid another friend to drive us up to Tallahassee. I didn't know how to how to register, I didn't know about dormitories, I didn't know anything whatsoever. So we rented a bed in a rooming house, not even a bed and breakfast, just a bed. We paid $5 a week and slept with six other guys. There were about four rooms on the top floor and one bathroom. No heat, and it got cold up there. They had a big old pot-bellied stove or whatever. We'd put paper in there and burn it, whatever we could to stay warm.

Years later I took my wife there and I said, "This is where I lived here on Calhoun Street." She said, "My God, it's a Salvation Army rooming house now. It is for homeless people." I said, "It was practically the same thing then, too."

I had to walk to school, down that long hill. I remember I found a place where it was a quarter for breakfast. There was a another rooming house where for 60 cents from 11 to 3 you could eat as much as you wanted to. They'd sit at a table with all kinds of people. Iced tea, all the vegetables you could eat, all the bread you could eat and they gave you one meat. A slice of ham or a piece of chicken.

But I still ran out of money in one semester, actually before the semester was over. I got a job at a grocery store cutting up chickens and making sausage. And I didn't eat sausage for 25 or 30 years after that because they had a bucket in the walk-in refrigerator, and every piece of fat that was cut off the meat, every scrap, everything was thrown into there . . . all leftover skin. I'd grind it and I'd have to put the sausage seasoning in it and I said, "I'll never eat sausage again." But I started eating it again because it tastes so good.

I did that until I cut my finger, and it was a really bad cut and they had to take me to the hospital and get sewed up. I said, "I'm not doing this." I ran out of money and came back to Miami. The only courses I took that semester that helped me was psychology and personality development. I think they came in handy all the years I have been a salesman. I came back to Miami and my mother threw a fit. "Oh, you've got to stay in college. You've got to stay in college." And I'm thinking, I don't have any money, you don't have any money. It is not for me.

The service: I think it was before I got my first job, the draft was still on. I felt I did my duty with the service because I worked while my three brothers were in the service. My three older brothers, Jack, Gene and Neal. And further more, I didn't want to kill anybody and I damn sure didn't want to be killed. My younger brother went and served later.

Before I was to report to the draft board, I was working for my Uncle Joe, delivered blocks of ice for refrigerators that were not electric. I worked with him about two weeks learning the route and it was time for me to take over and the boss says, "You can't wear those blue suede shoes here. You need steel-toed shoes." Well, I didn't have money for steel-toed shoes. So really on my first day on my own after my training they had a ledge there up off the ground about three feet, and I picked up the ice that was down on the floor and I threw it up on the ledge with the tongs. I threw it up and the tongs loosened and the ice fell out and landed on my toe. Landed on my big toe and smashed it. They took me to a clinic, not a bone doctor, not to a specialist. I remember laying on the table in pain and he took two long needles, not needles but they looked like needles and he was manipulating my bone and trying to put it back in place. And he put the cast on from the middle of my big toe all the way up to my knee. I went home and they gave me no medicine or anything, and I couldn't stand it. The pain was unbearable. The next day it hurt and the next night I couldn't take it any more, so my mother got me in the car and we drove over to an all night drug store called Robert's Drug Store, I think it was on Flagler or Southwest 8th Street. She took me in there around midnight or something and said, "He needs something for this" and we got some kind of pill that put me to sleep and helped me with the pain. Then someone said, "go get workman's compensation." I found out that my workman's compensation was about the same as my net pay check. I was supposed to take the cast off in four or five weeks and I left it on eight or nine weeks, and I didn't go back to the doctor.

Joe Brodsky came over and said, "That cast is falling off your leg, go back to the doctor." I said, "No, let's take it off." So Joe took one of those things that cut through limbs. He cut through the cast, took it off. I had a little piece of leg, really skinny after being in there eight or nine weeks. I tried to walk and fell down. There was no strength at all, so I had to be on crutches and a cane for awhile. Prior to that, the draft board called me to go down and take my military service examination before I had the cast off. They told me to notify them when the cast is off. And I thought to myself: oh sure, sure I will immediately. And I didn't notify them.

So then a few years go by and they send me the letter. In the letter it mentioned that if for any reason you do not think you should be in the service state below, and if you need extra space you can add a page unattached.

I explained about my foot: "I can't tie my shoe, I walk with a limp. I have severe allergies that cause pure water to run out of my nose all of the time." Which it really did when I had the job of sewing those straw squares from Haiti.

So between walking with a limp, and water coming out of my nose, and supporting my mother and father who didn't work, they didn't want to see me again. They sent me a card that says "4F", I do not think I would have made a very good soldier. But I do appreciate those who have served and risk their lives . . . even though I hate all wars. I love this country and all I have been able to enjoy in it.

After my foot injury, it took me about six months to find another job. I read a classified ad in the Miami Herald that said, "Young man wanted to learn a career from the bottom. Great opportunity." That's when I came to Harry Rich Carpets. It was here in the building I now own and run my carpet business out of.

Forty people applied for the job. I was interviewed as all 40 people were. Harry Rich had an administrative assistant, from Georgia and she asked me where I was from and I said originally Georgia. And I went to Edison and she went to Edison. I guess she was maybe 10 years older than me. She influenced Mr. Rich to give me the job. First janitor, warehouseman, truck driver and finally salesman.

Through the years, I would spend quality time with my dad. I was a salesman, I was in my 20s (when I'd take dad to watch boxing). Since I never saw my father in my early years, I used to work six days and two nights four months or five months a year. But during the slow time, I would get a half day off. That half day off I'd usually go pick up my dad, take him to lunch. He liked to go downtown to Richard's. Then maybe once every couple of weeks they had boxing at the Little River Auditorium, which was a movie theater and then they made it an auditorium for boxing. He loved it. I'd saved up money to buy a '56 Thunderbird. I would pick him up in that car and he was proud. When Muhammad Ali, who was known as Cassius Clay then, fought Sonny Listen, tickets were a fortune. But I knew how important it was for him. I got two tickets and we could barely see the ring from where we were seated, but he could tell his neighbors that he saw that fight and it was some fight at the Miami Beach Auditorium. Looking back, I am glad I took those afternoons off with my dad. I did it for him but it made me a better person.

After dad's stores closed, Mom became a checkout lady at a grocery store. It was Margaret Ann's, which became Kwik Chek, which became Winn-Dixie. On 53rd Street and Northeast 2nd Avenue at the Sable Palm Shopping Center. I had bought her an old, old car, stick shift, of course no air conditioning, window missing. So she could drive. On her lunch hour she'd take a nap and many days I'd go there and see her and see her asleep in the back of the car soaking wet from the heat.

But she was so exhausted from working eight hours a day, doing mine and brother's and my dad's ironing and cooking and mowing the yard. My dad sat on the front porch.

Joe Brodsky came over one day and my mother was painting the house with a mop because we didn't have a paint bush. And she missed a spot, and my dad from his chair and said, "Maitre, Maitre, you missed a spot over there." "Where Raleigh?" "Right over there, you'll see it."

She went over there with the mop, white washed it. Joe couldn't believe it. She was so devoted to her men. But that was our life.

Mom felt that you had to be the servant of the man, and the next generation didn't necessarily feel that way. She was very protective of her boys, which led to some tough times for the wives. She thrived on being needed. She was eager to cook and care for us men.

Mom's advice on how to get married:

She used to say, "Now listen here. Don't let liquor get a hold on you. It'll ruin your life. Raleigh let liquor get a hold on him, he just loved to drink."

Four of my brothers were alcoholics. One of them didn't drink for 30 years. Jim hasn't had a drink for 35, 36 years. Gene never quit drinking. My oldest brother, Neil, did quit until later on in life, four or five years before he died.

I said, "Neil, how did you give up alcohol after all these years? He said, "I drink Nyquil on the rocks every night. I have two glasses of it and I sleep like a baby and I get a buzz on."

Another motherly advice was: "Whatever you do Don, don't ever marry a woman that's been touched," meaning you have to marry a virgin. Well, that's pretty difficult, you know? But I found Gloria and did marry her, and she had never been touched. The marriage did not last long. Now that I look back I realize she was a good wife, but at the time I didn't see it that way because she wanted me to come home. After we got divorced we didn't talk for 14 years. She called me Horrible Don. And she was right, mainly because after we were married, I continued to date and drink and run around. I've been writing her recently and we still talk on the phone. We're friends.

After dad died I bought mom a home and would visit her most mornings before work. She would still collect rent and would have wonderful dinners for her family. She always had biscuits and plenty of vegetables and great iced tea. I would take her to church when I was in town. She loved the Baptist church and then we would go out for lunch. She was always appreciative for my time and attention. I loved my mom.

Brothers Don and Jim as youngsters.

Jim and Don as teenagers.

2. A CONVERSATION WITH DON AND BROTHER JIMMY

(At the 83rd Street store):

DON: And thank you, Jim, for wearing your teeth.

Jim and I hadn't been to a family reunion in years. It's the second Sunday in August, and we have a couple hundred cousins and second cousins. And we really go back to see just a few people like George Tanner Jr. and maybe Emma Jean and some of those.

I was sitting with one group of people and Jim was sitting with another group, and George used to work with me when I first started in business when I opened a little store in Atlanta, and I hired my Georgia cousin to work there. He saw that I was struggling and driving an old car and didn't have much money, but things were getting better.

So all these years go by, some 40-odd years, and he asked Jim, "How's Don doing?" Jim says, "Well, Don's doing good."

"Has he got any money?"

"Well he and his kids and family are worth about $20 million."

And George says, "Helen, Helen, pay attention. You know what Jim just said?"

"What'd he say, George?"

"Don, he's worth $20 million."

He says, "Jim, you're not doing real good are you? I can tell by the way you're dressed. No, they're not."

He says to Jim, "Have you got any money?"

"No, I'm only worth $10 million."

He says, "Helen, you're not going to believe this. You know Jim's worth $10 million?"

She says, "Yes, George, I heard him, George."

But we go up there just to hear him talk. It's fun to hear him and we love him to death.

JIM: Before we moved to Florida there are a couple things I can remember: Don and I were sleeping in a little frame house with a fireplace and we were all sleeping on the floor. An owl or a bat got in the house, and it scared the hell out of me. It must have been right before we came here to Miami, I must have been two and a half.

I remember playing with a coconut in the back yard in Dacula and dad was coming home from Miami. I don't think it was long after that that dad decided to move here.

What's funny is, my dad had a store there in Dacula, and Dacula had only one traffic light. Like if you blinked your eyes you missed it. He had a store there and he worked his whole family in it. He had done real well but he went broke during the Depression because the farmers couldn't pay him. It wasn't that they were crooked. They just didn't have the money because they couldn't sell their crops. That's why dad decided to move here.

When Don was talking about the time we were up there, we were in Dacula and we went to the same store that my dad had. It was still there. And the funny thing was, it had not changed. It was the same identical store. It had the same front counter, it had the same cash register. It must be a hundred years old. It had the same ladders to get up to the top shelf. Everything like that. And we tried to buy the whole store. We just wanted to buy the building.

At first we tried to buy the building with everything in it. The guy wouldn't sell it. And then we tried to buy the cash register, and he wouldn't sell it. Sure enough, not too long ago we get a phone call from one of our cousins and they said the owners were auctioning off everything. Sold the building and all the contents in it. My cousin said, "Jim, this is not going to be just in Dacula it's going to be statewide and it's been advertised. And you're going to pay top dollar to get any of this stuff."

So Don and I decided that we had our memories. We didn't want to waste our money on that old stuff.

JIM: First of all, Don and I are the best friends you could ever have. He's my best friend, but when we were kids we tried to kill each other. For some reason, I don't know why, but I was about as big as he was until he got to about 16. Maybe at the time a little bit crazier than him.

But I used to be able to beat Don. And when we were kids we used to get into terrible fights. Of course, he wanted to win because he was older. He was a tough little kid and could beat most of the kids in the neighborhood anyway. But he turned 16 and got real big, and I was 14 and he made up for every ass beating I ever gave him. He beat the crap out of me.

One time we were going to get into a fight, and this was when we were at the age I'm talking about when he could beat me, I wanted to protect myself. First of all, we drove to the railroad tracks. We were going to settle this and battle it out. And when we got there I saw a two-by-four and I started thinking, I can't beat him like I used to. And I picked up the two-by-four, and he says, "Jim, you're my brother, how could you? You pick up a board and you're going to use it?"

He says, "Let me have that board and throw it away."

I handed it to him and he took it and hit me in the side of the head and he knocked the crap out of me. My ear looked like W.C. Fields' nose.

And for about two weeks he didn't come home, and I couldn't find him. And I had a piece of rubber hose I was going to attack him with.

But, you know, we fought like that as kids but right after that as we got older we started becoming best friends. And I still had the same mentality. I used to box, and he was a football player, and I liked to fight and Don was more like he is now, the best salesman in the world. He could talk to people. But if somebody started screwing with Don, they had to go through me.

Remember when Candy's brother wanted to mess with you one time? I said, "Pull the car over, Dave, I want to talk to you."

He said, "What?"

I said, "You seem to be wanting to pick a fight with my brother. You know, Don's a good guy. He don't like to fight. But I do. Why don't we get out of the car and why don't you pick a fight with me?"

And he wouldn't get out of the car.

DON: Talk about the James Club.

JIM: I'm home at my mother's house in bed and Don comes home, I must have been 21 and he wakes me up and says, "Come on, I've got trouble over to the James Club. You gotta help me out."

I said "OK" and jump out of bed and throw some clothes on and we go to the James Club and his wife Gloria, his first wife, was dancing with a guy. Don goes right up and punches the guy. Now the James Club was full of people, and a lot of people were on the dance floor. Don punches the guy in the side of the head, and the guy goes flying. Somebody comes running toward Don, hit him because Don hit his friend but he didn't know I was with Don and I caught him coming that way and he goes flying. And a whole melee of fights broke out. You know, we're fighting everybody. And all of a sudden I look around and Don wasn't there.

DON: Tell about the police chief's son.

JIM: Is he the one you ran into the pole? Don grabbed him by the shirt and just kind of picked him up, 'cause Don was playing football and had gotten really strong. Picked him up and ran him into a pole. And he just slid down the pole. And I think it was after that you left.

DON: I ran out the door and jumped in the car. And what happened is, I had a choice: to wait for my brother and pick him up, or get caught by the crowd. I said, "Aw, the hell with Jim." I'm driving down and I look and there's the crowd coming after me. I had just gotten in the car and had just barely started taken off and Jim was in front of them.

He said, "Wait for me! Wait for me!"

I says, "Screw him."

JIM: I finally ran through some yards and got away. We had the best time growing up that know. We were poor but we didn't know it.

We had great friends. We were in a rough neighborhood because that's where my dad had to move because we didn't have any money. The Afro-American town ended on about 21st Street and dad knew if he opened a store there he would do well because he would give credit to the poor people and before they would pay any bills they would pay their food bill because they had to eat. And he did do well. He started making a good comeback, because he had done well in Georgia, but it took a long time for him. about 10 years.

JIM: I've been laughing at Don my whole life. He's without a doubt the funniest guy, and he's always coming up with something new.

Not too long ago there was a football dinner for Joe Brodsky, and Don and Joe were best friends. Of course I was there because Joe was a good friend of mine, too. And Don was one of the speakers. And when they called him they said, "And Don Senior is with us and is going to come out and say a few words." And Don Junior was the master of ceremonies. Don walks out there with sunglasses on and, of course, we're inside a building and you don't need them. And Don looks out at the whole audience, looks around, and he says, "My name's Don Bailey and I'm an alcoholic." He says, "Wait a minute. That's next week. I saw so many of my alcoholic friends out there I thought it was tonight."

The people are laughing like crazy and then he looks around and he says, "Ahh, I see my first sex partner in the audience." And I don't even know he's going to say this stuff. You know, he catches me by surprise. He says, "I see my first sex partner, and would my brother Jim please stand up?"

I'll tell you who was there: Jimmy Johnson, Lee Corso, all the famous people. And they are rolling on the floor. Some of these people that think they're great speakers, Don just killed them he was so funny.

A lot of things like that have happened over the years. When we were kids we didn't have any money but we liked to go to the Hurricanes' games like everybody else. And there were two ways we would do it. When I was younger, he used to sneak in by climbing over the fence and I couldn't do it. So he would climb over the fence, get in and go tell the guy at the gate. It was different back in those days.

He says, "Look, I want to let my brother come in because I have to go and I want to let him have my spot in here."

I would come in and he would go back out and climb the fence again. And we'd be both in there.

And then later when we were older we didn't bother to tell anybody. We used to just wait and when the guy who was taking the tickets was distracted we run and jump over the turnstile. Don would be first and I'd be right behind him. It would be boop, boop, and we just kept running right into the crowd. The guy couldn't leave, he's got to take tickets.

DON: What about the baseball stadium, Jim? Miami Stadium when the cars needed to be parked?

JIM: Somebody pulled up and we were outside. The guy says, "Where is there parking around over here?" And Don says, "Right over here. It's a dollar a car."

And the guy pulls in and Don takes a dollar from him and he starts parking cars along this building. I don't know how much money he made that night. That's when a dollar was a lot of money, 60 years ago. That was a pretty funny thing.

DON: Do you remember begging money from the sailors?

JIM: First of all, our parents had that grocery store when they came down here, and they worked 16-hour days. And Don and I were not raised, we just grew up. They were so tired when they got out of the store they went to bed and they were thinking we went to bed.

I mean, God, I was just a kid. I was 10 years old or younger and I'd be out until 1 o'clock in the morning and they wouldn't know it. And we used to go when the circus was in town at the fair and go down there, during World War II, and we'd go to the sailors because they were usually the friendliest, and beg for money. And they used to give us a dime and a nickle and stuff like that, and we could buy cotton candy and go on rides and go home at 3 in the morning and get up and go to school (laughter) with three hours sleep.

But I don't know anybody that was as crazy as us. But to survive that neighborhood we were fortunate because a lot of the people were criminals and went to jail and were killed. My family got us out of there. That was their goal because they saw what was happening. And I think I was 11 years old when we moved to from 22nd to 47th, which was a big move then because I don't think Miami went past 79th street. We made different friends and it probably saved our lives. Who knows?

Don went to work for Harry Rich as a young man. He told Harry, "I don't want to be your truck driver for life." He said, "If you think I have the potential to become a salesman, that's what I want to be. If you see that, that would be wonderful. If you don't see it I'd appreciate it if you'd fire me because I don't want to be a truck driver all my life."

By the time he was 21 he was a salesman. By the time he was 23 he was a manager of Harry Rich Carpet Company. There was a big writeup in the Miami Herald.

He's the best salesman that I know of. And I'll tell you, his son—they say the apple don't fall far from the tree—Don Junior is just like him. And he's very successful on his own.

After I got out of high school at 18 from Edison, I went in the Army two months after I graduated and I spent two years in the military police. When I got out, my dream . . . somebody told me if you can build a house and sell it, build another and sell it, by the time you build the third one you can have it paid for.

I thought, wow, that's a pretty good deal. I married a girl; her dad was an electrical contractor, so I was thrown right into the construction business. By the time I was in my early 20s I had a nice home but unfortunately by the time I was 31 I was divorced and my wife had a nice home, my ex-wife.

Then Don and I got together, and Don said, "I didn't trust your ex-wife, Jim," which was very, very smart. He says, "Now that you're divorced let's do it together."

And we did. We started doing it. And with Don's salesmanship and expertise it became . . . see, I was doing very good with houses, but if Don and I had never gotten together I probably would have done real good. But Don thought past all of that. Don said, "If we can get enough money and get a commercial lot and get into commercial building, we can really make some money." Well, I had never thought of doing more than houses. He thinks above that.

The first building we built was Williams Moving and Storage on 7th Avenue and about 129th Street. It's a big building. And we sold that and made $50,000. That was a lot of money back then. And that started the ball rolling.

Then I met a guy when I was working for my father in law. There was a guy that did all of his plumbing, an older guy, and I became real good friends with him. I told him, "Andy, my brother and I are going to town but our problem is we don't really have any money. It's hard and we need an investor that would loan us money."

So he said, "I'll loan you money at 10 percent," and that was a high percent back then. We said, "that'd be fine, we'll pay you 10 percent." And this guy really couldn't think ahead. All he could think of was that 10 percent interest.

What we would do is, we'd take what little bit of money we had and put a deposit on a piece of land. That's all we had. We'd go to Andy and say, "Andy, look, you're not real busy right now, we will give you a job building the building for us. What we need you to do is loan us the money to build the building."

So Andy comes over and he builds the building, pays for everything. We'd borrow enough from him to pay him back, I mean not from him, we'd get a mortgage. Yeah, we'd. go to the bank and get a mortgage.

DON: Free and clear building. The bank does not know we owe him money. All they know is these guys have a free and clear building. We get the money from the back and pay Andy back.

JIM: And we kept doing that for awhile. Then we had so many we didn't need Andy's money anymore. But he helped us a lot. We got all those lots along I-95 and built stores on them and the money came from Andy and he got paid back by the bank holding a mortgage on them.

It was things like that working together that we were able to figure out. Then of course his carpet business took off. I was a fireman, he was in the carpet business. He didn't have his own business when we started, he was working for Harry. We made a deal. He said, "I'll live off the carpet business," which was pretty easy for him. He was making a lot of money. "And you live off your fire department's salary." Which back then they didn't pay anything. I started off at $285 a month.

And he says, "Let's invest all the money in the property."

So I said "OK." It was a really good idea, it really paid off. But he was driving a Cadillac and I was driving a '39 Ford. Hah, hah, hah.

But if we hadn't done that . . .

We had some friends who were doing pretty good in building. But you know what they were doing? They would build a house, take the money that they made and live off of it. We'd build a house and take the money that we made and put it in the bank. We kept working, and they quit working.

DON: Yeah, we took the money and put it in the bank until we could buy another piece of property.

You want to tell them how I found you a wife?

JIM: Ha, ha, this is good. We used to have Sunday dinners at my mother's house. And they had a side yard and my other brother Jack and his family would come over and after we would eat we would take a walk through the neighborhood. I remember it like it was yesterday. And I'd been divorced for about a year and a half, and Don says, "Jim, I've got a real nice girl I want you to meet." And this was before we had gone in business together because I'd gotten divorced and my wife had taken everything.

And I says, "Don, I've been divorced a year and a half. See this piece of paper? I've got about four or five names on it."

He says, "Jim, you don't have a girl like this."

I said, "What do you mean?"

He said, "She's an airline stewardess, her father is a millionaire and you should meet this girl."

I said, "Nah, I don't think so."

He said, "Well, can I ask you a question?"

"Go ahead."

"How much money have you got in the bank?

I said, "I think it's $38.50."

He says, "I want you to meet this girl. Her dad's 80 years old. Ha, ha. He's a millionaire."

He introduced me to her. She was a friend of his wife's and they had known each other a few years. And we hit it right off and in a short period we were married. And 10 years later he passes away they settle the estate and her share of it was about $200,000 to $300,000 once the smoke cleared, and she sold the stock and everything.

She walked up to me and says, "Here, Jim, I've got this money. Here, take it."

This is the difference between the first wife and the second wife.

She says, "I see that you and Don really know how to make money. Put this into the building business" because we'd just started it. And that's what we did.

Now here's the salesman part of Don: He says, "Look, I introduced you. It's only fair that you pay me a commission. Ten percent."

DON: Ha, ha, ha, ha.

JIM: He wanted 10 percent and to this day I have never paid it and he still talks about it. Ha, ha, ha, heh, heh. You gotta get paid for your work, your talent.

DON: Can I add anything? First of all, Jim says we were really poor and I used to be just like Jim but I changed. I finally realized that I had some extra money. But Jim is still very thrifty and conservative. I'd give him my shirts . . . he's got one of my shirts on right now. Pants. Buy my old truck.

One time he was driving a truck that was 10 to 12 years old. I mean, we'd have to take a shower when we came home from the movie or something when we took his truck.

JIM: Ha, ha, ha.

DON: Last night we got free tickets to see an event and we almost didn't make it because he was finding a place cheaper to park. First he found a place where he could park free when he was a fireman. But they've put a building on it. He's been off the fire department 20 years and there's a building there now. Then we went around looking for a cheaper place.

I said, "Jim, Jim, it'd probably cost us $5. And if you'd take $5 from your $10 million you will have nine million nine hundred and something."

JIM: Ha, ha, ha.

DON: So he parked.

JIM: So any way, Don and I have been partners ever since and we've done real well together. We've got a lot of property that's owned by myself and him. I'm not bragging because I don't spend it any way, but I mean it's just a fact that things progressed the way they did. It was because we were both willing to work hard and do without things.

I used to go pick up rent from my tenants and I would be driving an old crappy car and they've got a Cadillac in the driveway. And they were renting from me. But they never got ahead.

We knew that to get ahead you've got to do something when you're born poor, and we were willing to do that. Both of us.

DON: Jimmy also when he inherited that money he gave 10 percent to the church. And on top of that he gifted them more money. And his wife will read something in the paper about somebody having a difficult time and she'll mail them a check. He read in the paper where there was somebody whose electricity was cut off and they wanted to condemn the house, and Jim read about it, and he's an electrician, and he went over there to fix her electric, carpet her house, paint her house and stuff. And we got over there and somebody already had started working on it.

JIM: Can I interject? First of all, I may not spend money, a lot of money, but I can give a lot of money away because Don and I believe in this life if you can't help somebody else, what has it been worth? He calls me, and I pick up the paper and right on the local page it tells about this woman having to sleep in her car because a storm blew over a tree and knocked her electrical service off the building. And her son had asthma and they had to sleep in the car with the air conditioner off.

I said, "Geez, I'm gonna go over there and fix that for her." And I jump in the car and go over there and I found out that there was an electrical contractor that beat me there and he was already working on it. But meantime I'm on my way home and I get a phone call from Don and he says, "Jim, did you see in the paper where there's a woman, her electrical service was blown off" and told the story I just told. And he said, "Would you please go over there and take care of that and our company will pay you for your work." I said, "Don, I just left there." And he really wasn't surprised. He told me that was a good thing I did, and so forth.

But anyway he hung up and gave her money,

And we have a guy that's been working for us for years, we've given him several cars, bought him a trailer home. We've helped two or three people or more get homes. I don't know how many cars he's given to his employees.

It's a funny thing. It sounds like we're cheap because we don't spend it on ourselves but we're not cheap when it comes to our fellow man.

DON: That's perfect.

JIM: And I like it that way.

I've been to a lot of places in the country. I liked to travel when I was younger. I've gone to the Pyramids and I've been to Rome, France and so forth. So I do things that make me happy but I don't . . . I'm the type of guy that if I can go out and get a real good dinner for $10 or $12 why would I go to Morton's Steak House and spend $8 for a baked potato and $40 for a steak? I'm not into that. Ha, ha. I was born too poor and I can't forget it.

Now Don has gotten over it a little more than me. Don will spend some money. I mean, he's not cheap with himself either.

DON: But I still drive a six-year-old car.

JIM: Yeah, but he doesn't go crazy with it. Your Wal-Mart clothes. I think most of his money goes to helping other people. He's got an employee plan that's a profit-sharing plan that goes to the employees. And as far as I'm concerned that's part of the reason why he's so successful, he's been so good to his people. They work hard for him.

JIM: We had another brother that was a sign painter. Don was looking through a magazine and he saw in Cosmopolitan that Burt Reynolds did this pose. And Don said, "You know, I'm going to put that on my building but I'm going to use my body." He says, "I think that will really draw people, especially women." Ha, ha. So he calls my brother Jack and told him what he wanted him to do. Jack was living in the Keys and he came into town and did that for Don and Don put it on his first building.

At the time I wasn't so sure it was a good idea, and I told Don. He says, "Who gives a crap if I've got a sign that says 'Don Bailey Carpets, Good Prices.'" He says, "But you know how many people will look up there if they see that and they may even associate that with Burt Reynolds?" He says, "Everybody will look. Everybody will look."

Once again this was his business mind, and he was right. He put that up there and it made him famous. I mean everybody in Miami knows Don just about.

I don't tell anybody—when people say, "Who are you?" I don't say Jim Bailey. I say I'm Don Bailey's brother. Ha, ha, heh, heh. And right away they know who Don is. When I die I'm going to be famous for being Don Bailey's brother. Ha, ha.

DON: And a lot of people know that he's my brother because I gave him six shirts that say "Don Bailey Carpets" on them. So he wears one each day, doing me a favor.

JIM: They're different colors.

DON: He does me a favor because he goes to LA Fitness almost every day. I mean, this guy's in the most fantastic condition—the doctor had to ask him to get off the machine because you can go all day long and all night long. He spins. I hardly know what spinning is.

JIM: They've got bicycles and it's got a lever on it where you can make it where you're going up a mountain and you've got an instructor and these instructors work you hard and it's for an hour. And I get on that bike, and he says, "We're going up that mountain." He says, "Push it to number 10," you know. And people walk out all the time. My doctor told me, "Even though you're 75 you've got the heart of an athlete." 'Cause I've been doing it about four or five years now. I do it four times a week.

DON: And he wears those shirts. And he belongs to another gym. And people are asking, "Do you work for Don Bailey?" He helps me out. He always has helped me out.

When I got real successful very early and he was still a fireman making no money. And he has never been jealous. Never.

JIM: I'm too proud of him to be jealous.

DON: But I'll be honest, I was jealous of him because his first wife had great tits and mine didn't have any.

JIM: Ha, ha, ha, heh, heh, heh.

DON: I was very jealous.

JIM: I offered to share.

JIM: He had reason to be jealous of me but I never have been jealous of Don Bailey. You know why? He's the first successful person I guess—other than my dad, but my dad went broke and died broke—but Don is the first successful person in the history of the Bailey family that I know of. On our side of the Bailey family. And I think it's something to be proud of. And I was always proud of him.

If our dad hadn't moved us out of that neighborhood, we probably would have been killed or in jail because I'd already gotten in trouble as a juvenile. I was in junior high and a couple of us went out and stole a car and went joy riding. And we got caught, and they sent me to Kendall Reform School. We went all the way to Jacksonville and they caught us on the way back, at Titusville. We went up there and realized we didn't have any money, and what the hell were we doing? We were going to California. We were crazy. And we turned around and started coming back and we hit a chicken truck. Ha, ha, heh. We had chickens all over the place. Ha, ha. That's how the cops caught us.

But I did listen to the judge. I went before the juvenile judge. He said, "Jim, let me tell you something. You're just a kid. You're 15 years old. If you were 17 you would have gotten a criminal record. If you ever wanted to be a policeman or fireman . . ." And I always thought about it when I was a young guy. And he says, "You could never do it because they wouldn't hire you. But if you turn your life around right now and don't get in any more trouble, this will not show and nobody will know about this."

And I did. I knew that I had to either stop acting that way or not get caught any more.

Ha, ha, heh, heh, heh.

So I decided it's better not to do it because you can always get caught. But anyway, that's how I got on the fire department. I told them I had no record and they could find no record. They do a thorough check on you but they keep the juvenile files closed, which is good.

DON: I think Jim's right. If we had stayed in that neighborhood we'd been in jail. Or we would have . . . I mean, so many of the people got shot and killed. I mean, Charlie, Thomas, Willard, David, Nicki, Joe, Red died in prison, Buddy, Johnny. These guys are dead or got shot during a robbery. And we were right there among them.

And I've been in jail for breaking and entering. What happened is, I used to deliver stoves and kitchen cabinets, and once every couple of weeks I would go pick up what I'd delivered on a Friday and I'd go pick it up on a Sunday because it's new construction. And they usually would leave the house open. So then we would give it to my uncle Joe Wood or my uncle Tom Parks. And they would buy it and they would resell it.

So me and Jimmy and Johnny Garcia were drinking one Sunday and Johnny has me start driving up to Fort Lauderdale beach. So he gives me directions and I said, "John, this is where we delivered that stuff Friday." He said, "Yeah, we're going to pick it up today." So Jimmy's in the car, he had no clue. He was already on probation. The place was locked up. So either me or Johnny hit the window, and it was empty and we went in and got that table top stove that fit in the back seat in the car. And we got back in the car and started driving away and we see a guy coming and hollering at us. And we said, "Ah, screw him." But he took the tag number down. We went out continuing partying and drinking. I guess I was 18 or 17. So the police stopped us in North Miami. This happened in Fort Lauderdale. They said, "What's with that stove?" They took us to jail and they interviewed us separately. But before they interviewed us separately, while they were doing some paper work, Jim says, "Listen, tell them I wasn't there because I'm on probation." I said, "No problem."

So I go in, Jimmy says I wasn't there. They just picked me up. And they come in and I said, "It was just the two of us." And they go and see Johnny and he says, "Yep, three of us." And Johnny knew not to mention him. So the guy came back and said, "Listen, you're lying Don. There were three of you. And the man that took the tag number said he saw three of you."

I said, "He couldn't have, there were two of us."

And he says, "One of you is lying."

I said, "Who said there was three of us?"

He says, "John Garcia."

"I says, "He's a habitual liar."

JIM: And he really was.

DON: Except he was telling the truth this time.

JIM: It was two of us against one of him, so they let me go.

DON: And I was in jail a day or two and so was John. And I got three year's probation.

DON: Jimmy thinks a lot, but some times he doesn't think. I'll tell you one of the times he didn't think. When we go to the movies, first of all, we feel what they charge for movies and popcorn is way too much money. We're talking about as recently as last week.

JIM: Ha, ha, hah.

DON: We say you spend $10 to get in the movie, and you spend $25 on popcorn. It's crazy. And we'll go with our wives too. What we do is—my wife never knew it, and now she won't go to the movie with me—I'd buy two tickets, you know, and there'd be four of us. And I'd wait until it gets a little crowded. Come on in, get the popcorn, and I'd shuffle them in. And there's four of us and I've got two tickets. Never got caught. Now Jimmy and I go to the movie and I buy one ticket. Or I buy two and only give them one. And Jimmy goes in and I say, "Wait for a crowd, wait for a crowd." He says, "OK."

Now we'd never been caught. This time we got caught. And so he waited for a crowd, and I'm waiting around and I'm not paying attention and I see him walking in and my eyes got this big. And he got nabbed. He came out and says, "They caught me." I says, "Jim, wait for a white crowd. Not a black crowd. But he went in with a group of blacks."

JIM: I'm the only white person in a group of 10 people and naturally they spotted me. Ha, ha, ha.

DON: Also, we'd go in with my wife and his wife and my son Brett, when he was younger, and we'd buy one big popcorn. And we'd bring our own bags, and I'd stand there at the end of the counter and we'd fill up the bags and I'd say, "Jim go back and get another one" so we could fill them up again. And we'd buy one big Coke and bring our cups from home

JIM: We'd get one Coke and one popcorn but they would be the large refillable's because most people don't refill them.'

DON: We figured $50 deducted from your $10 million would still be $9 million 9 hundred . . .

JIM: Poor people would come in there and buy their kids all separate little bags of popcorn and separate Cokes and spend $50, and we'd spend $10 and four of us would split it, our wives and all. We had to train them. They came along pretty quick.

DON: We'll have to stop doing that some day, but not any day soon.

JIM: We're only in our 70s.

DON: I kind of calmed down because of my job. But we hung around with the roughest, meanest criminals. One guy killed his own brother in our neighborhood. Guys that lived only three or four houses away, always fighting like Jim and I were. And Daisy Mae, and I'd be ticked all the time if my name was Daisy Mae. But he was a rough SOB. And he killed his brother Jack in a fight and had no regrets.

JIM: Daisy only had one eye. He lost his eye. If anybody said anything about it he'd go after them and try to take one of their eyes out. He was crazy. I didn't call him Daisy, I called him Mr. Mae. Ha, ha, ha, ha, ha, ha, ha.

DON: That's our neighborhood. That's our neighborhood. It wasn't Mr. Roger's neighborhood.

Recent photo of Don and Jim

Don and Jim as kids with ladies.

3. BIRTH OF THE BILLBOARD

Burt Reynolds posed nude in Cosmopolitan magazine about 38 years ago. Of course, it caused quite a stir. A friend, Hank Fineberg, who now lives in Boulder, Colorado, came to my house for dinner and he pulled out a photograph where he was laying on the floor nude in the Burt Reynolds pose. We all laughed. It was just the funniest thing. In the exact pose.

And I said, "Geez, Hank, are you going to use this in your advertising?" He was in the carpet business, too. He was in South Miami and I was in North Miami. He said, "Are you kidding? Of course not, I'd be the laugh of the town. Are you kidding? This is a joke."

I said, "Are you sure?"

He said, "I'm positive."

I said, "Then do you mind if I use it?

He says, "Are you kidding? You'll be the joke of the town." He says, "Go ahead and use it."

I didn't have much money then, I didn't have enough to have a sign painted. My carpet store at the time was the equivalent of maybe a six-car garage on I-95 and 98th Street in Miami, and maybe one or two customers coming in a day. I'd only been in business a short time.

I had started with a $5,000 loan. And a friend of mine, Jasper Williams, gave me some inventory to put in the store, and I was doing no business. Fortunately my brother Jack was a pictorial artist. He painted outdoor signs before they would do it on vinyl and hang it. He'd pull himself up on a billboard and paint it, and you have to really be an artist to do that. I asked him if he would paint a billboard sign with me lying like Burt Reynolds on the side of my carpet store.

He said, "Are you kidding?" I said, "No, I'm not kidding. Look, there are a hundred carpet stores in Dade and Broward and Palm Beach counties. They all look the same. There's no flair with any of them. I happen to be on I-95 with 200,000 cars going by every day. If I put that up, they will remember this carpet store, believe me, good, bad or indifferent."

Well, he came over to my house one night, took the photograph of me laying on a shag carpet. It was Bigelow's Curryvale, it was a big seller. I was naked. He took the photograph and I still have a copy. Then Jack painted the sign on the building, and a day or two days later women just started coming in. I think I had 20 the first day. Before it was good for two, three, four in a day. But in no time there was a steady stream of people coming in and buying.

But then, I get a notice that 300 people from a church group signed a petition and took it to the Dade County commissioners and said they want it taken down, no nude guy should be laying on I-95 or in this community. The sign got to stay and I was happy because I was heading down the road to failure without it.

Not long after that, I had three billboards in the Keys because my brother Jack had started a billboard business in the Keys. He was having trouble renting the three signs so I rented them with the rental information below so maybe other clients would rent them. I had two of my sign and one of my second wife Johannah, who was a model, absolutely beautiful.

Later I outgrew that store and we moved to 14831 NW 7th Ave., and even though it wasn't on I-95 it was on NW 7th Avenue and I put my second sign up there. Business was very good there so I opened in Miramar and put the sign there on 441, which had a lot of traffic. Then we opened one on Broward Boulevard in Fort Lauderdale years later and I put the sign there. And years later I put one on Martin Luther King Boulevard in Fort Lauderdale between Sunrise and Oakland.

I got tremendous publicity when I put the Miramar sign up. We had to go to the Miramar commissioners and Vicki Coceano was mayor and she said, "The sign cannot stay until he puts a tuxedo on. He's not going to lay naked in Miramar."

To my good fortune an Associated Press member was in the audience at that commission meeting and he put it out on the Associated Press. A few weeks later my lawyer Gordon Taylor came in and says, "Don, here's your picture in the paper."

I said, "Yeah, I saw it in the paper."

"You mean you saw it in Korea?"

I said, "What do you mean?

He says, "My son is stationed in Korea, this is in a Korean paper."

And it went all over the world. And it went into the national trade magazines, Floor Covering Weekly. It just took off, and it's amazing.

Rumors went around that it was Burt Reynolds' body and my head. I even started the rumor some times as a joke. They said, "Is that your body?" I said, "No that's Burt's body and my head." But most people knew the real story . . . Some people started believing it and it circulated around and somebody in the press got a hold of it. They said, "It's Burt Reynolds' body and Don's head." It was investigated and Burt Reynolds said, "No, that's not my body."

Through the years I have gotten a lot of press about the sign. I was in some national magazine and I sent my wife to Lohman's Plaza to buy 10 or 12 copies but they were $19 a copy. And I said, "Buy one." Basically what it was, they published monthly about a major city—Seattle, San Diego, New York, Jersey City—the highlights, the most interesting things to see in that city. Sites to see, things to do. Sure enough of the things to do in Miami is see the nude carpet sign.

One time they paid me to park my truck that has the sign on the side at a store in Aventura Mall. They wanted me in their catalog. All they wanted me to do was sit in the truck and have the truck parked while some of their models run by. They had a guy with a video camera and a photographer. The still photo was of the models starring at the sign.

There was one sign on my building at 83rd Street but it was taken down because I didn't get a permit. But we have my truck parked out front and a big truck parked out front and both trucks are wrapped with the sign.

There's a sign on 116th Street and I-95. We own the building and that one that still gets 200,000 viewers a day, going southbound. And you can see it northbound but not as well. Then we have one on 7th Avenue and we still have the Miramar one and one on Broward Boulevard and we have one on Martin Luther King Boulevard.

I'd say I get comments about them everywhere I go. They see my truck that has the Don Bailey sign, they honk their horns, put their thumbs up. Some times the middle finger up, if I cut them off in traffic.

Of course I dine out a lot and go out to lunch a lot and park that in front. I've had people come into a restaurant and say, "Who's Don Bailey? His truck's out front."

Tremendous recognition. I was voted number one in Florida for the tackiest sign. I loved it, I agree with them. It's tacky but it gets me business.

And I'm trying to think of another tacky idea.

And then the Florida Power & Light Company put out a survey a few years ago. It was number one, the best billboard in Florida. The very best billboard in Florida for getting attention. Number one.

So I've been number one at both ends of the spectrum.

The photo used to make the original billboard.

The original sign.

4. FLOORING BUSINESS AND REAL ESTATE

FLOORING BUSINESS:

It wasn't like I came back from FSU and went to work for Harry Rich Carpets. I looked for a job for six months and couldn't find one. It wasn't so easy to find a job back then. There was an exporter downtown on the river, and I would have loved that job. But I couldn't type fast enough. Everything went fine until I typed.

Then I saw a small loan company where they needed somebody to go and collect, which my brother Jimmy actually did. But they didn't hire me either. I thought I'd get that job.

I went on interviews but they were few and far between because nobody was hiring. So I started looking in the Miami Herald classifieds. That's why I still take that paper, I don't care if it goes down to one page, because I bought my real estate out of that paper. At the beginning I bought all of my real estate out of the Miami Herald.

After six months of looking I saw the Harry Rich ad. I fortunately got that job. Unloading carpet, me and one other guy, with no forklift and no loading door. It was really tough, but I didn't think it was tough. I was so happy to have a job.

I started working for Harry Rich Carpets in 1953. I thought I'd saved enough money for four years of college but I hadn't and I came back home. Tallahassee was so lonely, especially when you're broke. I told my mother that I saw an ad in the paper about a young man wanted to start a career and learn the business from the ground up. I was going to try to get that job. She started praying, "Let him go back to college." She was a church-going lady, Baptist, everything was about prayer. I said, "No, I'm not going to do it, I don't like college."

I got the job. Forty people applied. He hired two people. I started working as a truck driver's helper, and when I wasn't doing that I was doing the janitorial work. Then the truck driver, Norman Ward, quit and I became the truck driver. They had another truck driver before they put me on the truck. I noticed that he would go out at about 8:30 and come back a little before quitting time, about 5:15. It didn't matter if he had six deliveries or 15.

So when I became the driver, the job was more efficient. I didn't care if I had 20 deliveries, I would deliver geographically and I would be back at the store by no later than 1. I could be going to Miami Beach, Hollywood, wherever. When I got back I would do my janitorial work.

But when I was in the store, there were customers hollering to be taken care of. Mr. Rose, Gil Murray, Bernie Weinkrantz, the sales crew, were all busy. I got to take care of people because they demanded somebody talk to them.

I started selling them, and they let me continue because I was selling the less expensive stock, the rugs and the tile and not the wall-to-wall carpet. Wow, then they gave me a commission check. And I said, "Damn, that's more than I make as a truck driver." I would make even faster deliveries and come back earlier. I really started selling a lot. One of the salesmen, Gil Murray, got jealous because I was outselling the other two. He went over to Harry Rich and said, "You know, he's losing sales. I saw three people walk out of here today. Harry, you gotta have those customers wait until I can take care of them." Mr. Rich came up and talked to me. "You can't sell any more. Maybe occasionally you can sell a box of tile or a $29 rug." When he was telling me this story, one of the customers came in that had walked. And they tried to give her to one of the salesmen. The customer said, "No, I want this young man to take care of me. He was very polite." I made the sale. It was a big sale, too.

That same day another customer came and said the same thing, "No, I want him to take care of me." A few days later the third customer came back. I brought it to their attention. "You know those three people that I lost? They all came back and bought."

I was still the truck driver until a few months later when they moved into the new building (the one I currently own) from 5,000 feet to 18,000 feet, and they promoted me to salesman. I tore it up and I became the top salesman. I was top salesman every month until I became the store manager, then I became the general manager and then the first vice president. I was so hungry for money. I'd never had money before. I saw how much money I could make selling and I kept a record of it. I knew how much I made every day.

I continued to work there and I enjoyed it. I had been there 14 years. I was getting bonuses then at the end of the year that almost equaled my yearly pay.

Harry Rich liked to tell a story to that when he retired and left New Jersey at 39—that he sold his three top employees 48 percent of his business and they paid for it out their bonuses. He would give them their bonuses and they would use the bonuses to by the stock. He said he wanted to do the same thing here in Miami and he promised me that would happen. A few years went by and nothing happened.

I was talking to my brother-in-law and he said, "You're working hard and you can't even spend time playing with your kids because you always work and are exhausted." And I saw my kids playing and I was too tired to move. Don Junior was saying, "Come out and play, dad, come out."

We were visiting on a Sunday afternoon at my brother-in-law's house and the kids were playing and I couldn't stand up. I couldn't get off that couch. I'm working six days, 8 til 9 o'clock. I started thinking I've got to find out what's going on with this business. So my brother-in-law says, "Ask Harry Rich if he's going to sell you part of the business."

I came in and asked him if he was going to sell me part of the business. He said, "Yes, yes." So I went back to my brother-in-law the next Sunday and I said, "He's going to sell me the business, it's finally going to happen."

My brother in law said, "When?"

I said. "When?"

He said, "Yeah, when?"

"I didn't ask him when."

So that next Monday morning I went in to see him and said, "You know, Mr. Rich, I really appreciate you making me feel better by telling me you're going to sell me stock in the business, but when?"

And he says, "You're getting to be a pest."

I said, "No, my brother-in-law asked me this question and I was embarrassed I didn't follow through with the question,"

He says, "When? Maybe next year."

I said, "I know what he's going to ask me: If maybe next year but if it's not next year, when?"

He said, "You know something? Maybe never."

I said, "Oh, OK, that way I know where I stand."

That's when I made my plans to depart. One of the salesmen, Mike Soen, had been saying, "Don, you and I sell more than anybody in the store. We can open our own store down the street."

A carpet installer that had worked here, had left three or four years before and had become very successful and was renting a building on I-95 at about 80-odd street and he says, "The three of us will be partners. We don't have to pay rent. I've got inventory left over from the Fontainebleau and from other installation jobs. We can each put $5,000 in."

I didn't have $5,000 so I borrowed it, and Expressway Carpet Sales was an immediate success. I worked there four years with my partners. One partner did nothing except get drunk and come in at 11 and leave at 1 and bitch about everything. He was loud and aggressive. I read the prose, Desiderata, that says, "Avoid loud and aggressive people, they are vexations to the spirit." It also mentioned to try to go through life peacefully and do things for others. And I thought, man, this is not happening for me. I'm dealing with an alcoholic and he's mean and he fires people and he breaks up families. He is so difficult to be around and he is making me miserable. So I'm out of here.

I told my brother Jim, "There's a place on 98th Street at I-95, it's like a six-car garage. I want to move in there and start my own carpet store."

We scraped up a little bit of money each and we put a low down payment. The building was $45,000, I think we put up $2,500. I moved into that little place.

What happened then, I was struggling. I lost just about half the money that we had the first month, and the second month we broke even. Then a friend of mine, Jasper Williams, had a carpet installation and sales company called Carpet Systems and he had a lot of remnants he couldn't sell. And he said, "Don, I'll give them to you on consignment. This way you've got inventory. You don't have much inventory." This gave me merchandise to sell.

When I left Expressway Carpets, the customers came with me. My ex partner finally moved to New York, where he was born, and he opened Expressway Carpet Sales there.

When we started Expressway Carpets we ran an ad on Labor Day and it showed pictures of the owners in it. We were all well known from different restaurants and lounges around town. We were swamped with people. You've never seen so many people.

I had to call my wife in to come help sell. We were swamped 'cause it was the first warehouse-to-you operation. It was like a Levitz; you could take it with you. Or we could deliver it tomorrow.

And there weren't many people back then selling carpet. There was basically Miami Carpet and Harry Rich and Carpet Mart. So things were going pretty good. The one partner wanted me to go with him everywhere to entertain him. He had another business of installing furniture and I would go everywhere he went, and it didn't have anything to do with the carpet. It was going to Texas, Boston and Chicago discussing his other business that he owned himself. He liked me around because he wanted me to be his drinking partner and court jester. I got tired of it. We opened too many carpet stores and all of a sudden we weren't making the money because of thievery.

I remember things had gotten our of hand when we were in Dallas. We had a store in Dallas. He said, "We're going to Houston tomorrow."

I said, "Why are we going to Houston?"

He said, "I've got a chance to do some furniture installation. It'll be a big deal."

I said, "I've got customers in Miami I've got to take care of, I've got a schedule that's all set for tomorrow and the next day."

He says, "Nah, you're going with me to Houston." We talk a little while and he passes out at the table, at Steak & Ale. I flew back to Miami, the hell with it. My business was beginning to dwindle because we spread to New York, Texas and other cities.

Some other things happened, and when he got back to Miami he wanted to go to lunch at the Mousetrap and he says I didn't go with him and that wasn't right. Like I was disobedient.

I said, "Look we're equal partners here. I've got as much to say about this business as you do."

He said, "That's what you think"

I said, "What do you mean?"

He says, "I own that building and you don't have a lease. I can go lock it right now. There's nothing that says you can be in my building. You need to do what I say."

And I'm thinking, "No I don't." So that's when I started making plans to leave him. And it's the best thing I ever did.

When I left Expressway I formed a new partnership with some guys who were doing very well in the flooring business in South Miami. I remember saying, "I don't even want to make any money on this. I don't want to get rich any more. I want to be able to pay my car payment, pay my house payment and take care of my wife and kids."

At that time that was only about $250 a week to cover my payments. I put in $5,000 and I think they put in $5,000. I got half and the three of them got half. But we all drew an equal amount out a week. We decided we would draw $250 out a week. My best salesman from Expressway Carpets came with me, Dick Bartlett. Thank God and I'm forever grateful to him.

We sat there 60 days, phoning everybody we went to high school with, everybody we ever sold anything to, anybody we ever met, and that's all we did. When we hung up the phone, before we made the next phone call, we hand wrote an envelope and a letter thanking them for their time and to please remember us when friends or relatives need carpet, and we enclosed a card and mailed it.

Still no business. I lost about half the investment the first month, and then we broke even in the second and started making a little money in the third.

I would sometimes run home for lunch exhausted, I'd work from about 7:30 or 8 in the morning until 9 at night two days a week and the other days until 6 or 7. So one time I was complaining to my wife, Johannah, "You know, this doesn't seem right. I'm working full time, they've only been in the store one time in a year. They were getting the same draw from the business. I said, "I've got to buy them out or do something."

She says, "When?"

I said, "Next year, probably."

She said, "No, do it today. Buy 'em out today."

I said, "I think it will, I can't take it any more."

This time I own the building and they didn't have a lease. I could lock them out. That was the lesson I learned.

So I called my partners. One of them says, "The business is going to be worth a lot of money in a few years." I said, "Well, how much do you think it's worth?"

He gave me a really big figure. I said, "That figure is perfect. So why don't you buy me out at that figure?"

"Oh, no, we couldn't pay you that much."

And I said, "Why not? You want me to pay you that much."

He said, "Well, the business is nothing without you. We don't know any of your people."

I said, "That's the point. You want to make it fair? I'll buy you out."

He says, "Well, what about such and such amount."

I said, "You know I don't have any money. I'll give you that amount but I'll have to give it to you weekly. That is all I can do."

So I paid it off in a year or year and a half. The payment was the same as their draw, so it was like having them as partners for another year and a half. But I never had to use what my ex-partner used on me: I don't have to pay you anything, I can lock you out. I wanted to handle it fairly. By handling it fairly, I kept those guys as friends.

My friend, Hank Fineberg divorced Harry Rich's daughter after I started my business the first time with my two partners at Expressway Carpet Sales. He came to work for me at Expressway. We had sample rooms, and there was a hallway and one door was across from the other door where each person who stood in the doorway could see each other but the customers behind the wall couldn't see what was going on. He asked me to check on a price. It was a new sample and he said these people are very interested. He was very serious. And I liked to play jokes. He said, "Just give me a price." And I said, "It's going to take a few minutes."

He said, "OK. I'm showing them a few other things." I went back to my doorway, I didn't go back in the room, and I said, "Hey, Hank, I've got the price." And he came to the doorway and he looked across and I was standing there naked.

Now he had to go back and talk to those people. He just stood there and stared at me, chuckled underneath his breath, tried to stifle a chuckle and a laugh. And tears came to his eyes, and he was able to maintain his composure and went back and sold the people carpet.

Hank moved to Boulder maybe 10-12 years ago, but we remained close friends. He called me one night about 10 o'clock and even though it wasn't good news I felt honored that he would call me. What happened, he's been in the carpet business out there and he was feeling tired and he went to the doctor and after an examination the doctor said, "You're heart's in very bad shape. You have six arteries blocked and I have to do open heart surgery right away." And he was getting ready to be operated on and he called me. I thought that was really nice that he wanted to talk to me before he went under.

I told him, "You know, it's going to be fine. Once they put that needle in you before you count to 10 you'll be out and when you wake up it will be all over with." He said, "Yeah, I'm not afraid." Hank had his operation and thankfully is recovering well.

Carpet Road Shows:

When I was with Expressway Carpet we started going into small cities to sell carpet. This is how Wal-Mart started also. Every week we'd run an ad in the local paper and sell carpet. We would do so much volume. My partner at the time had a piece of property in Naples. We took a bunch of carpet over there, ran an ad and sold like crazy. I could write really great ads because I was taught by Harry Rich.

So on weekends, we were selling a ton of carpet. We were only open two days. I'd work five days here and two days there and take the other guy with me, or hire somebody to take the money. We finally hired a lady and her husband. And we were doing good, and it slowed down a bit but still doing great and the partner said, "Let's move to another town." And we did. We sold lots of carpet in Fort Myers and Sarasota.

I remember one time, I worked in our warehouse until 6 o'clock at night, rented a U-haul truck, loaded it up, and got on the road at 8 or 9 o'clock at night going to Sarasota. It was hard work and long hours, but we were making a lot of money.

Then the stealing started, people started keeping the cash. Our salesmen, our installers kept the cash they collected after the job. We just couldn't control it. Even when I started my own business, I would do the road shows, until my bookkeeper told me one of her friends saw our truck pull up and unload some carpet at her neighbor's house. What salesmen were doing was selling carpet from the truck. I didn't have the staff or inventory control. If something was missing I never knew it. Not like today where if there's three inches missing, we know it.

So we finally stopped the road shows and went back to what we could control.

When I left Harry Rich after 14 years, I was a great salesman but not a great businessman or even a good businessman. To me it was just selling, selling, selling. Harry Rich never showed me a financial statement. I didn't know the overhead in a business like the 40 other bills you have to pay without buying carpet: Forklift repair, paying the forklift off, the rent, the insurance, the lights. Sometimes I'll sign 40 checks, none of them are buying carpet. It's all this other costs that had to be paid before we made a profit. The percentage of profit is what I figured out to stay in business and it was my most valuable lesson.

During the Harry Rich era:

Lee Rice, who was Mr. Rich's administrative assistant, who called me the son she never had, took me under her wing and wanted to train me. She saw how hard I worked. She was from Georgia, I was from Georgia and I was always polite and worked hard.

She took an interest in my life. One of the tips that she gave me was when I would have a date. She said, "Where are you going to take her?" She said, "That's a nice place. Now have you been to that restaurant before?"

I said, "No."

She said, "Well, you need to go there before your date."

She was the lady. She wore gloves until the day she died. She wore a hat. She dressed like something out of Southern magazine.

She said, "You need to go to that restaurant first and find out where the ladies room is. That way if your date wants to go to the ladies room you get up, you pull her chair out and you walk her to the ladies room."

And I said, "OK."

And she said, "You also wait by the door until she comes out and you escort her back to the table."

Then she said, "If she wants to go to the bar first and she's not finished her drink by the time the table's ready, you carry her drink and yours over to the table."

She covered many details about etiquette and manners that I needed every day. I was a pretty rough guy but wanted to learn.

She was very instrumental in getting me, a 25-year-old guy with four or five year's experience to be the senior vice president of one of the largest carpet stores in Florida.

We started having to wear ties to work. She watched me for a week and said, "You're wearing your dad's ties to work, aren't you?"

I said, "How do you know?"

She said, "Well, some of them are stained. Some of them have been out of style. What you need to do is get some nice ties. If you'll give me $20 I'll get you some nice ties."

Now I'd seen ties two for a dollar. You know what I mean? She got six ties for me. Six ties $20? And I wasn't making that much money then.

She said, "Yes, Don, these are stylish."

And today, 50 years later, I have one of them. It's a Madras with different colors. I have it as a souvenir from her.

But all along the way she trained me. She said, "You had a nice sale here. Did you thank the lady?"

"I sure did."

She says, "Well, how did you thank her?"

"When she left the store I said, "Thank you very much.""

She said, "Did you walk her to the car?"

I said, "No."

She said, "You need to walk your customer to the car. And if it's a lady you open the door, and you stay there and close it and thank her. But what I'm talking about, did you send her a thank you note?"

I said, "No."

She said, "I'm going to get you some thank you notes. When you make a sale here's what you say: 'Dear Mrs. Smith, Just a note to thank you.' Put that in quotes and underline it, for the business. 'I appreciate it very much. Please remember me the next time you, your relatives, your friends need carpet.' If you can remember anything that was personal, you can add that."

Well, those thank you notes got me more business because nobody at that time sent them.

She's been dead maybe 10 years. But January 17 was her birthday, and on her birthday long after I left Harry Rich she got a dozen roses from me. On Christmas I sent her a nice gift. And she always wrote me the nicest thank you note. She would write in beautiful cursive. She would describe the gift and the color of the gift and where she was going to use it. She was so good to me.

For a time, Harry Rich treated me like a son. He treated me better than he did his own son David. And David was brilliant. David came to the carpet store after college and analyzed what was going on and went to his dad, and his dad should have listened to him. He observed every person at each location.

David went to his dad and said, "Dad, you have about 12 managers and they all have assistants. The only one working is Don Bailey. The other 12 you can fire and let their assistants do the work, because that's who's doing the work now." I think Harry Rich's feelings were that he was making tremendous money. We used to have 50 customers lined up to get in when the store opened Monday mornings. Not every Monday, but when we had a big sale. And he figured he could afford it and still made a lot of money and so he kept everyone on the payroll. The problem was, he kept them on the payroll when the business slowed down after I left.

Everything David came up with, he shot down, so David left. Even though he's younger than me I always admired him because he was a good businessman and always analyzed things. He should have been paid a huge bonus for his analyses, but nothing was done. And eventually there were new carpet businesses opening up and business dwindled at Harry Rich. Eventually, they went out of business, Harry Rich died and I bought the Biscayne Boulevard location from David.

REAL ESTATE BUSINESS

My brother Jim and I started investing in real estate during all the years I was in the carpet business. We kept the properties small, usually only 5,000 to 7,000 feet so we could afford them whether they were rented or not. Most of our properties stayed rented. We would pay off any mortgages or borrowed money first and then invest in another property with any income that came from the building. It took time and we both sacrificed to build this venture with the thought of leaving our children with income-producing properties that would take care of them one day. People told us to leverage and buy more, but we were not comfortable doing that, so steady and sure we bought properties and rented and bought more.

I did make one large blunder. A friend of mine I used to work with at Harry Rich when I was a manager, and he was the manager of the acoustical tile department. He had built some nice projects and made some big money, including a flea market on 7th Avenue. It's still there. We were talking one night and I told him my older brother married somebody pretty wealthy and they had a big piece of land on Bird Road and they're trying to sell it.

He said, "Bird Road, that'd be a great place for a flea market." I went to a bank to get credit and they wouldn't loan me $10,000. I was going to put a deposit on the land and he was going to borrow the money to build the building. I said, "I can't do anything, I can't even get $10,000."

He says "Well, I have a banking connection and we'll go to them, and they know the success I've had, and we'll go in 50-50 if you can get your brother to sell at a certain price."

So we bought two blocks on Bird Road. There was the Lindsay Lumber Yard, 40,000 feet, there was the Winn-Dixie, 30,000 feet, there was a barbecue place, a pizza place. There were all kinds of buildings but there was no rental income because the rent went to the land lease. There were 16 more years to go on the land lease. Then all those buildings came to us.

We knew all that going in, but there was also one big piece of land that we knew we could build a flea market on. So we went to the bank and got my older brother to talk to the other four people that inherited the property. Their bank could carry the mortgage for awhile and we borrowed enough money to build a 50,000-square-foot flea market. And we built it.

After the flea market opened, I had to park three blocks away. It was absolutely mobbed, like Aventura Mall is now but in a flea market. We had a girl on a red velvet swing, a beautiful girl on a little swing 30 feet up in the air. We had spotlights, and it had a great grand opening.

It was so good that my partner came to me and said, "Don, you know you got 50 percent and you didn't really do anything. We got it on my credit, we got it on my expertise, I handled the building of it. It seems unfair." I said, "What are you saying?"

He says, "I should have 75 and you 25."

And frankly it did seem unfair. So I gave him 25 percent and he's now 75-25. And business is booming.

All of a sudden after three months the world ran out of gas. There was no gas. The first gas shortage. So when I went out there after the world ran out of gas I could park right at the front door. Nobody was there. Week after week it was the same.

I went in and talked to the different merchants that were left, because everyone started leaving. And I got each one and said, "Why don't you give something away that's cost or below cost. So I got the produce guy to give away tomatoes at low cost, and I got the tennis shoe guy to give 'em away, and I got this one and that one. We had 50 tenants in there. We had a cafeteria and they were selling hamburgers below everything. Don Junior and Johannah and Bobby and I went out there to all the major stores along Coral Way and Bird Road and SW 8th Street, and we had fliers with the prices and we put them under windshield wipers. We would start at 8 or 9 in the morning and we worked til late in the afternoon. We did that for four or five Sundays, and it didn't even work. People just weren't driving, you know? I was using all my gas coming from Miami Shores.

Then I find out, even though I'm only 25 percent owner, if there's a default and my partner doesn't pay, I have to pay the whole 100 percent. So he moved to California, address unknown. I still tried to make a partial payment until the banker called me in after I made three or four payments. I wanted to keep my credit.

He says, "This little bit of money you're paying is not helping you. It's going to ruin your credit anyway. You may as well stop unless we can get somebody to buy it."

We got a realtor who kept claiming that he had it rented or had it sold. He was lying to us. He wanted to string us along until we couldn't go any longer with the bank and then he bought it. That's what happened. He bought it under a friend's name for like 40 cents on the dollar. Today it's probably $50 million. You've got to remember what the dollars were in the mid '70s compared to what they're worth today. We had maybe two and a half million in it.

What made it so good for him, he could hold on 16 years and all those tens of thousands of square footage that goes for two blocks, plus our 50,000 square footage, it's all his. The income is tremendous.

I finally called him one time, I said, "Sam, you never did have a car dealership go in there like you said. You never had a yacht dealer, you never had investors from New Jersey. You never had any of those. I know what you did. I didn't know it then, I figured it out later. Years later. The least you can do, 'cause you own so much property that you got the same way you got mine, apartments, condos, you need to buy carpet from me. You're worth $50 million on my dime."

So for a short period he and his son bought carpet, then he stopped. But what I learned was, I was stuck with the whole bill. And I would have been killed financially, I would have been bankrupt. Everything would have been gone. Mike Gardner's a friend of mine, his dad, Jim, owned a bank. Mike was ready to take it all but his dad says, "Listen, is this going to work out? First of all, they paid high interest, 18 percent. We're going to get a lot of interest from these guys. We're not going to come out so bad. We're not going to take everything Don owns. He's going to have to pay me so much money and we'll give him five years."

It was a struggle because it was a lot of money. But I paid it off and it never ruined my credit. To add insult to injury, that is when Johannah, my second wife, left me, when I was in the depth of despair. And she made me sign whereas she wouldn't be responsible for this debt when we got divorced. So I signed, which I was glad to do. She was the mother of my three children.

Here's what it taught me: That I will never buy another piece of real estate unless I can afford for it to sit empty without renting it or selling it. So that became my philosophy. When I bought again, it was a small warehouse that I could afford for it to sit vacant, in case the world ran out of gas again. I could pay it from the other properties I had. So I graduated from a 3,000 s.f. to a 5,000 s.f. The Biscayne carpet store is 18,000 feet and I've got another 16,000 but most of my warehouses are 5,000 to 10,000. It also taught me about dealing with a bank and really reading contracts. That's the reason I pushed my youngest son into law school. And he excels in contract law.

As for leverage, that's not my cup of tea. My accountant used to tell me years ago, "You need to get mortgages on all these properties and buy more property."

I says, "No, I don't want it. First of all, I will be paying a lot of interest. That makes someone else rich. If I have extra money on hand it can go for things I do not need. Let me pay this building off. And then I'll work on the next one and so on.

That's when I stuck to my guns. He says, "You're the only one doing it. Everyone else is on leverage."

And you know what's funny? He did talk me into going with him and his accounting partner on some orange grove property in Orlando, on leverage, and we lost it. And I said to him, "Do you like leverage now?" He said, "You were right. I'm not going to suggest it any more."

So I stuck with it and as a result everything we have is paid for. Thirty buildings.

Except we did buy one recently but the borrowed money came in house. So it is borrowed from the income of other properties. And that's the only one and it's a small mortgage.

Don in ad with wife Johannah (left) and Audrey Crawford.

Building that Don originally worked in and later bought.

Don busy building his carpet empire.

5. CRAZY STORIES AND LESSONS LEARNED

The reason I don't have much of a Georgia drawl is because I've been here 72 years. Sometimes the Georgian accent it more noticeable. My wife will tell you about my mispronunciations. Like Jimmy Johnson does, "Go ooon and ooon." I say the same thing, "Go ooon and ooon."

Instead of saying "where," I say, "Whur's my shoes?"

My youngest son says, "Whur? What does that mean . . . ? Do you mean where, dad?"

One time when my 24-year-old was about 14, we were going down to the Keys and I bought him a voice recorder and I forgot all about it. Coming back from the Keys a recording was on. And I said, "How much longer are you going to play that? I don't want to listen to that. I can't listen to that hick any more. Who is that hick?"

He said, "That's you, daddy."

I said, "That's not me."

He said, "Yes it is. I recorded it on the way down."

I could not believe how I sounded.

When Al Hinson was probably 10 years old, my son Don was a few years younger. We went on vacation I took Al with me, and Don and Bobby. Al, I thought of him as a son since he was like 9 or 10 years old.

He's 54 today and I still think of him as a son. Actually I like him better than any of my kids 'cause he's nicer to me. But anyway, he's a wonderful guy.

Back when he was 10, he was old enough to hit the ball with me in tennis and I was new at the game. We were in Cashiers, North Carolina, on the tennis court hitting and swinging and I came up really hard and hit myself over my eye and it opened up the skin pretty good. Blood poured out. I couldn't even see. I'd open my eyes a little bit, and I tripped and fell. There was a ledge three feet up.

When my wife, Johannah saw it, she said, "We're going to the hospital."

I said, "Not right away."

I got on the phone and called the hospital and told them I cut myself. And she said, "Come in and get it stitched up."

I said, "How much are stitches and what's the visit?" I didn't have money back in those days. I had money, but not a lot of money. So they told me how much it was and I says "No, no."

She says, "It'll leave a scar if it don't come in."

I says, "No, no."

So I cleansed it and called down stairs to see if they had a nurse or doctor and the guy asked what's wrong and I told him and he said, "Why don't you push the flesh as close together as you can and put a piece of tape over there so it'll heal together?"

My wife and I pushed it together and she put a piece of tape, and I left the tape on til it fell off. There might be a little scar, but not significant. When I hit myself in the head, Al's such a gentleman, he didn't laugh. But years later he says, "I was crying with laughter inside, especially when you tripped."

We used to go on annual carpet trips to conventions with 200 people. One of the guys who owned a carpet mill said, "I want to hire you just to hang around. You make me laugh."

We were in Europe and one of the things that happened was, everybody was drinking and having fun and dancing, and I thought it would be a good idea if I danced with a cooked pig with cherries in the eyes and an apple on the mouth.

So I tried to pick it up and the waiter at the restaurant said, "No, no. You can not do that. Why do you want to do that?"

I said, "I want to dance with the pig."

"No, no, that's against the law" or something like that.

I said, "I can't dance?"

He said, "You can't dance with a pig in Europe."

I said, "I dance with pigs all the time in the United States. As a matter of fact, I married one."

But I had picked it up a little bit and the meat started falling off. So the only thing I would have danced with would have been the head.

But that brought the house down.

The another time, I started a Conga line. It was kind of boring, because I was the only one that had a few extra drinks. But everyone joined the Conga line and there was like a 100 people in it, and there was like 150 still sitting down.

So they had a flower arrangement. What I did was pull my pants down and stuck it between my legs like it was growing out of my ass. And I got at the end of the Conga line. And as we came through again I was shaking those flowers. And that brought the house down.

I like to make people laugh. I like to laugh.

I used to like to spend time with my youngest child, Brett, on Sundays. So he was very interested in a game and I figured what is it, 20 bucks, 40 dollars? That's great. So we get in the car and go to Aventura Mall and we go to this place that sells games.

And Brett said, "Do you have such and such game system?

And he says, "Yes I do, I have a few left."

Brett says, "I'll take one."

I says, "Hold up, Brett. I always like the price before I tell anybody I'm going to buy something. And that's what you need to do. Don't be like your mother, who doesn't care, doesn't understand, and they'll just charge the hell out of her." I says, "By the way, how much is this?" And the clerk says, "This is $300 plus tax."

And I looked at Brett and says, "Are you out of your freaking mind? Who do you think you are, a prince? Do you think I'm some kind of king with money or I have oil wells in Texas? I'm not spending that. I used to work more than a month for that."

And so he says to the clerk, "I apologize for my dad. He's not supposed to have coffee. And when mom's not around he drinks coffee, so he drank too much coffee. Plus he has a little bit of a hangover and that's why he gets crazy."

He was around 12 and he said, "If you'll put that away I'll be back here with my mother and we'll buy it later."

And we calmly left and I gave him a lecture all the way home about watching dollars and buying less expensive games. A few hours later Donna and Brett left, went back and bought it, with my blessings.

The coffee had worn off by then.

When I used to dress like a nun—well, I used to dress like Elvis Presley too—the nun was the one that got the most laughs. When I dressed like a nun, two or three times I went to the Bayshore Whale and Sail, where friends of mine hung out, like Ben Pumo. He used to be a carpenter and he owns about a thousand warehouses. A great guy. Mike Gordon would be there, from Mike Gordon's restaurant. But Mike, his glasses were pretty thick, almost like Mr. Magoo.

I was there and Mike came over and said, "Sister, can I buy you a drink?"

And I said, "Sure."

So he bought me a couple of drinks. A couple Friday nights later I did the same thing.

"Sister" said Mike Gordon." How are you?"

"Fine."

"Can I buy you a drink?"

"Sure."

He got closer this time and he looked real close.

"Dammit!" he said. "You're Don Bailey! Why are you dressed like that?"

I says, "So I don't have to buy my own drinks. You know, I just went through a divorce."

And he laughed.

A lot of laughs came from the other friends at the bar. That was hilarious.

Here's how the Christmas cards started. We were on another carpet convention on a cruise ship. There was a couple hundred carpet people and their wives. There were dinners and breakfasts and a few beers, and there were laughs. But no real crazy fun.

And so I got me one of those teeny bathing suits, what do they call them? Thongs. And I put three wash cloths in it. I also had a Rasta wig, you know, the braids, the dreads. I also put that in the front of the thong. Looked like my pubic hairs hung down to my knees. I put the Elvis wig and the Elvis sunglasses on, sideburns, and I have a pair of red and gray disco shoes that have about four-or five-inch elevation. That's what I wore out there to the pool on the ship.

The snapshots going off. Everybody was taking photographs. Everybody laughing and so forth. To add to it, there was toilet paper hanging down between my buttocks.

That's all they talked about for the next three days. Everyone thought is was so funny. Around Christmas I said, "Donna, we ought to send this out as a Christmas card." So we did. And people started saying, "What it going to be next year?"

So for over 20 years I use different themes—I've been Don King with the hair sticking straight up in a bikini. It's always the pose, sideways with the wash cloths. I did Willie Nelson, Rasta Man, Santa Claus, just the beard and the red thong. When I hit 70, I came up with a great idea but Donna didn't think it was. I said, "You know, when guys get 70 I should wear just regular white, and instead of putting the three wash cloths right up front, let me have the bulge in the back, because that's what old guys do."

She wouldn't do it, she wouldn't send it out. Donna takes the pictures in front of our Christmas tree.

One of my very best friends, the late Joe Brodsky, was in Dallas with Jimmy Johnson, Dave Wannstedt, Butch Davis, all those guys, and I would send him Christmas cards all those four or five years he was there. And he'd show it to all those coaches. When Butch Davis came to the University of Miami, they had a big reception with 400 or

500 people there, cocktail party, and people were lined up and he was shaking hands and I came up and I said, "Butch, I want to introduce myself. I'm Don Bailey."

And he said, "I want to be on your Christmas card list."

I said, "How did you know?"

He said Brodsky showed all the coaches and half the players. He showed it to Troy Aikman and the guy they call Moose.

"Everybody knows you," Butch said.

I said, "In Texas?"

He said "Yes, in Texas."

The problem is if we leave somebody off, they get really upset. We were at a University of Miami party the other night and Todd Roy, who used to own my favorite restaurant, The Depot, said, "How come I didn't get a Christmas card this year? What'd I do wrong?"

He made a big deal about it. Anybody that doesn't get one, they'll call us and say, "Where's my Christmas card?" We have so many requests we haven't kept a very good list. People move and they don't send us a card and so we don't have a new address.

But that's been fun.

I give a speech maybe every six months or so. My speeches are unusual and they're comical. The evening for Joe Brodsky was one of my best. And I thought it was being videoed. But the guy with the camera, a real religious guy, cut it all out of the video that contained my speech because he found it offensive. It was offensive . . . . But very funny.

On the dais was Jimmy Johnson, Norv Turner, Lee Corso, and other people and they gave humorous toasts to my good friend Joe Brodsky. But when I got in front of the microphone, Don Junior says, "If there's any children in the audience, you need to take 'em out now. And if there's any women or men easily offended, you'll need to leave the room because he's not going to hold back."

So I had my suit on, a little dignified, I had glasses like John Lennon used to wear, but they're blue and I put them on and when people saw those glasses they started laughing. I says, "My name is Don Bailey, and I'm an alcoholic." And I looked around and I lifted my glasses and I said, "Damn, that's tomorrow night. The reason I said that there's so many people in the audience that goes to Alcoholics Anonymous with me, I could swear I was at an Alcoholics Anonymous meeting."

I went on to say, "Listen, we're honoring Joe Brodsky. And what is so coincidental and it's amazing that the very first person that I ever had sex with was the first person Joe Brodsky had sex with. And that person's in the audience tonight. Will my brother Jim please stand up? Where are you, Jim?"

Jim gets up like he's a celebrity and starts smiling and waiving around the room. And I said, "You know, we didn't have sisters. It was in the late '40s and early '50s, and we used to dress him up and he was very nice about it. Nobody's holding it against you." Jim was so happy, he said, "Because everybody came up to me afterwards and wanted to meet me." He knows how to take my jokes. He has been around me a very long time.

I said, "They want to do more than meet you, they want to M-A-T-E you."

In the speech, I went on to say that the main thing Joe and I had in common, we were both premature ejaculators.

I said, "I remember the first time I met Joe Brodsky was at Robert E. Lee Junior High School. I was 15 and in the ninth grade, Joe was 23 and in the eighth grade. I just needed a father image and he took me under his wing and we've been friends ever since."

People were roaring. We run into people today—that was 15 years ago—and they say they'll never forget that speech.

Even on Donna's 40th birthday I had a speech, and on her 50th birthday I had a speech and on her 60th I had one.

The Miami Touchdown Club has me speak every now and then. I introduced Gary Dunn one time and I got so caught up making people laugh, I was on a roll, and I forgot I was supposed to introduce him. I thought it was my show. So Gary hollers out, "Hey Don, introduce me, dammit, this is not your night this is my night! Just say my name and let me get up there. You get the hell off the stage."

I said, "Give me 15 more minutes, Gary, relax. You're not funny. They want to hear funny."

The other time, Joe's fraternity from the University of Florida had a gathering. It was groups from the '50s, '60s, '70s, it was a pretty good group. They were celebrating their fraternity as they do every three or four years. They asked me to be the guest speaker, in Miami, mostly people from Dade, Broward and Palm Beach County, and some friends were also invited.

So when I got up, I started this way: "My name is Don Bailey and I'm a lesbian. At least I think I am because I like everything I think the lesbians do. I like kissing women. I like going down there to no-no land. And I just love women. So I'm pretty sure I'm a lesbian." And I went on from there and they roared all night.

Most people who have heard my speech before start laughing before I say anything. Or I get requests not to speak. I do not mean to offend, just want to get laughs. Life needs more laughs.

REAL ESTATE LESSONS

You know, when you're in your late 20s and early 30s, you're more into working and not dreaming. I mean, maybe you're dreaming of making a lot of money one day. But I met a guy whose name was Colin Dixon, he previously had been a motorcycle policeman. He and I had a lot in common, and my wife and I went out with him and his wife and we were talking and I was telling him how happy I was selling carpet for Harry Rich. After we socialized for several months he said, "Listen, you're not going to make any money unless you make capital gains. You can make something nice to live on and you might have a good retirement, but if you're going to make some big money, you're going to need some capital gains."

But I didn't know what capital gains was. I had no idea. I said, "How do I make money from capital gains?"

He said, "Well, let me tell you how I started. You know, I was getting ready to buy a house and I started thinking that if I bought a duplex, all I'd have to do was come up with was enough money to put down on a house and the other side would pay the mortgage. So I started living rent free.

I started thinking, so why don't I buy another duplex? I need a little bigger place. So he bought another one. And he bought a triplex. He said, "I kept thinking and thinking." And I flashed back to something my dad had told me many, many times.

He always said this: "Don, you've got to think. All through out your life you've got to think." He said, "If you're not going to think, if you're not going to use your brain, you might as well have two assholes. Otherwise, what's the brain for?"

I'd say he would say that every two or three weeks. "Have you used your brain? Otherwise you might as well have that second asshole." So it started sinking in, but it didn't sink in for a long time.

I went to my brother because I didn't have enough money and I said, "Jim, why don't we put money together and buy houses and rent them?" And that's the first thing we did. The rent was paying the mortgage. I said, "Why don't we buy a duplex?" Taking Colin's advice we bought a duplex. We bought a place on 46th Street that's a house in front, a big apartment over a three-car garage. We could make that garage into another apartment and we'll have a triplex.

And then we bought a place on Miami Avenue, a four unit that had a garage and we made a fifth unit out of that.

We had the property but we had to put a bathroom in and we didn't have enough money to get a permit, but there was a crazy old country guy by the name of Andy Collins and he said, "Do you know if this is connected to the sewer?" And we said, "We don't know anything about it. We don't know if it's sewer or septic tank."

He says, "Well, I can rent a machine, dig up Miami Avenue and connect you right there. They've got a sewer running right by, or septic tank or something."

So anyway he actually dug up Miami Avenue on Saturday and Sunday and connected it to the sewer, filled it back in. We'd all have gone to jail, had we'd been caught.

We were happy with our property but it was only paying the mortgage. We weren't getting any money.

You always have to remember, real estate is not always a great investment. You have to be patient. After a while, we decided to invest in warehouses.

We put a deal together where I put a mortgage on my free and clear house. I bought a house in Miami Shores for $16,000, with real estate going up I got a $35,000 mortgage.

I put my portion up and we built a warehouse on I-95 and 125th Street and we tried to rent it for a year and it didn't rent well. We had $50,000 invested in it, and we had it less than a year and a half and we sold it and made $50,000. There again, $50,000 doesn't sound like much, now, but in the late 1960's it was.

So that's how we got started in real estate.

I'm just guessing, but between me and my brother and property that I've given to my wife, property that I've given to my ex-wife, a property that I've given to my kids and property that my brother has given to his, I think we have something like 29, 30, 31 properties.

My second son, Robert, oversees this. It's a full-time job. He is the best property manager we have had. We had an accountant, paying him about $12,000 to $15,000 a year. What I asked him for years and years was: I need a monthly statement on how much we're making or losing on each one of the properties, I need the rent roll, who's paying and who isn't. I never got it. We needed someone who could attend to our properties full time.

When Bobby took over, the first month he had me a statement of all the buildings, how much each one brought in, the rent roll, how much taxes are, how much we've got in the bank. And he made them all LLC's. Doing it perfect. A wonderful job. So we've got a lot of buildings. We didn't always pay them off; we've got them under control. We've had one building that was about 10 times what we paid for it, and a lot of them five, six and seven times.

What happened, we would get a building and once the mortgage was being paid for, we've accumulated a little nest egg and we use that money and buy another piece of property. So this is a process of about 40 years where we got 30 buildings. We don't get one every year but that was our goal. But we only buy bargains. Only bargains.

It helps if you marry your real estate broker and she helps and supports you along the way. We rarely just go for a drive. She drives and I look for real estate. This means turning around in high traffic areas, sitting in the heat as I step off the building or patiently waiting as I talk to people about the next deal. If she complains I say, "You like to eat don't ya?, You like vacations?" Donna rarely complains and has brought me incredible good luck.

I think I got my compassion for the working man from my family being so poor, and we didn't get any help from anybody. I always thought, there's got to be somebody out there that's got more money than they need that can give it to someone who needs help. We had some lean times. But it never happened.

When I started working for Harry Rich, I saw what a very generous man he was. He gave to Goodwill and to Channel 2 and many charitable organizations but never directly to an individual. I was working with people who were struggling—guys that were installers or they were helpers. I said, "If I ever make a lot of money I want to help those hard-working guys who just get by but help me make money." When I started making decent money I started helping my dad and mom. When I'd get my bonus check, which was once a year, the first one I got was overwhelming because I'd never seen that much money at one time. After I cashed it, I took my mother and dad—they didn't have a car—I took them to the grocery store where she later worked as a cashier. I told them to fill up as many carts as they want, get anything they want and I'd pay for it. So they did. And I bought them a car.

I think the first person, other than my parents, I helped was Gene Gibbs. I went into business for myself, and Gibbs was the warehouse guy who worked so hard and looked after my inventory. He worked harder than anybody. One day I look back out the warehouse door, which overlooked the bus stop, and he's standing there and I came back 30 minutes later and he's still there waiting on the bus to go home after work. So bought him a new motor scooter.

Months later I see him leave on his motor scooter in the pouring rain. I say, "You know, this isn't right." So I bought him a brand new Mercury. And we tied a big red bow on it. We parked it in the warehouse.

He came in and said. "Whoever owns this car needs to get it out of here, I've go to make cuts and do some work."

And I said, "Why don't you read the card?" He read it and couldn't believe it. He was overwhelmed. So when he took the car home that night, a neighbor was there and his wife said, "I believed in him. We can't even afford groceries for the week and he goes out and gets credit and buys a new car." The neighbor said, "He probably didn't buy the car. It's a blessing from Reverend Ike." You know, if you send Revered Ike $5 you'll get a blessing. And this is his blessing."

Gene said he came into the house and said, "Where's Mae? She says she thinks you went out and bought that on credit. I told her it was from Reverend Ike. Have you been sending him $5 every week or two?"

He says, "Reverend Ike my ass, Don Bailey gave me that car."

Maybe a year or two later, he didn't say a word, his wife was the maid for somebody who worked in my office. I heard she said they were losing their house. So I found out what he owed, and he didn't owe much, he'd had it a long time. So I paid the house off for him.

When my business got slow, and I had two warehouse guys and I went to Gene and I said, "I'm going to have to let the other two guys off, you might have to work a little harder. I can't afford them with business bad and I have to let someone go."

And he said, "Don, let me leave. I'm only here because of you. I'm getting Social Security now, my wife can get Social Security, and there's a little house in Georgia left to me by a relative and I want to go back to where I was born in Georgia. I would never leave here, but now that you need somebody to leave, I'll leave." And that's what he did.

After that, over the last 20 years I have bought 15 cars and given them to employees that needed transportation. Some were like new, one was my daughter's car. Rather than trade it in on another car I bought it from her and gave it to someone who needed it. I put a down payment on my mother's house and Johannah's mother's house. At one time I had five people that were living rent free—didn't pay insurance, didn't pay mortgage payments, didn't pay real estate taxes. Two were in RV's, big ones, one was in a big trailer.

One young guy I helped made the front page of the Herald: Corey McCall. When he came to work for me, he was around 12. He said he needed to make some money. His dad left his mom and he was going to buy her a birthday cake. I said, "What can you do?" He said, "I can sweep and clean up around the garbage can." And I gave him the money. When he left I said, "I bet he's not buying a birthday cake." Sure enough when I left work, there at the bus stop was that kid with a big cake box on his lap. I could tell he was a good guy. So I had him work whenever he came by.

When he got to be about 15, he lived in Larchmont Gardens, which was a high crime area. He said, "Some of my friends are stealing cars."

I said, "Corey, if you stay good and honest, when you're 16 I'll buy you a car."

"Really?"

"Just don't give me any trouble or the deal's off."

At 16 I bought him a car. A few months after that, we were talking and some of his friends were still getting in trouble. I would take him home some nights. I would teach him how to figure square yardage from the sizes of the room. I taught him how to figure it faster in his mind than in a computer. And he learned.

He was really bright, and I hated to see that mind go to waste. He was working hard. I said, "I'll tell you what I'm going to do. If you'll stay in school and graduate with good enough grades to go to college, I'm going to pay your way to college. And I'll pay for your books and your food and you'll have another car to drive around."

Well, he didn't get into trouble. And when he graduated from high school, I did just what I promised. That's what made front page of the Miami Herald. The article was more about him being an inspiration to other kids. I think he's in the Club of 100 or 500—older students that take a younger student under their wing. He was kind of passing along the tradition of helping the younger kids, not financially but spiritually and giving them hope for their future.

I sent him to college and he came back and worked for me briefly and is now back in school getting his masters in business management.

During one hurricane, a guy that works for me had a brother who was in the recording business and had all this equipment. It was worth more than $6,000 because it was new. In the hurricane somebody broke in and stole it all. So he's out of business—that's his business. So even though he didn't work for me, his brother did and I heard the story and I felt bad for him. I said, "You know what? Tell him I'm buying all his equipment but I'm not buying new because I know the difference in the price, like a new car and a used car." He came back and it was $4,000. And I bought it for him and, you know, he never said, "Thank you." Never.

But here's the way I feel about it: I'm not going to let a few guys along the way that's not appreciative keep me from giving to people. And what did my heart good is that Don Junior is helping a guy through college.

A guy came by, I guess he was about 15 or 16, and looked Don right in the eye and shook his hand and wanted a job. And Don said, "You should be in high school."

He said, "I am but I'll be dropping out."

Don says, "But what about your parents?"

He says, "No, my mother and father are dead."

"So where do you live?"

"I live over four blocks away and I sleep on the floor, I don't have a bed."

And Don saw the potential, the firm handshake, look you in the eye telling you the truth of his situation.

So Don told me about not having a bed, so I went out and bought a bed and delivered it to his house. And he started working for us part-time, and Don says, "You're bright." He got a tutor for the kid. And his grades started going up; his senior year he started making A's.

So Don didn't tell anybody. I found out by accident. The difference between me and Don is, Don does it and doesn't say a word. I do it and don't stop talking about how great I am. And if I'm going to do something I want somebody to know about it as an inspiration for other people to do good for the poor.

I manage to find enough people without them seeking me out. I have a budget that I allow to give away. And I prefer giving one on one.

This last sales meeting we had, Don stood up and says we're going to start giving every quarter or month or semi-annually a trophy and a cash reward for our most outstanding employee regardless of position. It doesn't matter. Good at teamwork, does their job excellent, everybody that excels in all phases. I know there are several of you that think "It's me, it's me," because I sell so much, and the other one says "because I work so hard." But it's going to our warehouse manager Leshon Kelley.

And then he proceeded to tell the story about Leshon Kelly. When Leshon was about 15 years old, and now he's probably 28 or 30 or so, Juan Comendiero's wife, who's a school teacher, called Don and says, "I want to do you a big, big favor. This might be the best favor that's happened to you in a long time. There's this kid that's a foster kid. His mother and father left him when he was like in the third grade, fourth grade. But he always had a cheerful look, he's smart, he looks you in the eye when he talks to you, he shakes your hand firmly and he was never any trouble. He's in the 10th grade now at Central High School and he needs a job, he needs to make some money. You need to hire him. Just do me a favor and hire him."

And Don did. Now this kid comes in, he's about 6-4, Rasta dreads, and you would think he's gonna wait for you outside and either beat you up or rob you. But he turned out to be the softest, the sweetest guy, the nicest person you'll ever meet. So basically he worked til he got out of high school and at 18 you have to leave the foster home. He was living with like 15 or 16 people in Little River, and at 18 with no money and no place to go you're out on the street. So Don had a small apartment house off Biscayne Boulevard, so he gave him an apartment to live in. There's only one room, and he lived there and he took a bus to work or rode his bike to work. And Christmas came and I started thinking about, well, he's not going to get any Christmas gifts. My wife and I went shopping. I asked him what he would like and he said, "Well, I'm interested in music." I says, "What instrument?" He says, "drums."

So my wife and I went shopping and bought him a few gifts, and I dropped my wife off and I picked him up and we went to Sym's Music and I let him pick out a drum set. That drum set barely fit in that little, small room.

So what happened, he loved it, was happy and then there was another apartment that opened up and was bigger and Don gave him a bigger apartment. And he excelled with us and kept the best warehouse. We had no problems. I have a townhouse and I gave it to him to live in free. About five, six, seven years ago he moved into a two-story townhouse and he pays no rent, no taxes, no insurance, he just pays his electric bill. He deserves it. I think I've given him three cars over the last several years and one just recently. And I try to give him money now and then.

One time I set up a savings account for him and started with a thousand dollars. I send him on vacation to Jamaica and so forth. He's like a son to me and I love him dearly and I'm going to take care of him as long as I'm alive.

Running out of cash:

When I was a kid, I started working at 13 or something washing cars and mowing grass, things like that. Then in the summer I used to work after school. I always saved my money. If I didn't hide it, my dad would pluck a little, my brother Jim would pluck a little. I knew there was a little plucking going on.

So I had my Edison yearbook and I had twenties in these different pages. I figured, who's going to look at my yearbook? But the thing is, $20 was not $20 in the early '50s, $20 was $200. If I took a $20 it would last me two weeks. Gas was 19 cents a gallon, or something. All of a sudden I noticed it was getting down to nothing. I couldn't believe it when I ran out of money. Then I couldn't get a job.

It made me save. That's why I had the Holy Five. And my dad, even though he didn't save, he taught me how to save. He says, "Don, you're doing these odd jobs and you're spending all of it. We're going to take you downtown and start you a savings account."

And so he took me downtown and we opened it with $5. He said, "Now what you want to do is save $100. That's you goal."

I said, "That'll take me forever."

He said, "You'll do it."

It did take a long time and when I got to $100 I was so proud. I went to him and said, "Dad, I've got a hundred bucks in the bank."

He said, "Good, now leave it there. You need a thousand." I said, "That's impossible."

He said, "No it isn't. Put whatever you can week after a week."

And after a while it was a thousand and I kept doing it and I got to $5,000. I saved and it bought me my first house, $16,000 for a house in Miami Shores.

That shows you what $5,000 was worth back then. That house eventually went on the market for about $300,000.

I never missed a day's work at Harry Rich except for mumps. I had the mumps.

First of all, back then it was so hard to find a job, you wouldn't keep the job if you missed. Harry Rich let us know right off the bat.

We called him Mr. Rich; nobody called him Harry. I'd always be the first one there and one of the last ones to leave. Usually Harry Rich was there when I got there. He asked me, "What time did you get up today?"

I said, "I had to be here at 8 so I got up at 7."

He would say, "I lived two hours longer than you did today already."

I says, "How?"

He says, "I got up at 5 and went for a swim in the ocean, I went for a walk."

He says, "You need to get up earlier and live longer."

I thought, you sure don't have my hangover. For 14 years I was never late and never missed a day. And I came in with the mumps with about a 105 fever. When he saw me he says, "Don, there is an exception to the rule. You need to go home and come back whenever you are better. I don't want you infect anybody else."

But here's how strict he was: He would give you a half day off, my half day was Thursday. You go to the dentist, you get your haircut, you buy your clothes, everything. When Don Junior was born, I had to pick him up one day that wasn't Thursday, so I went to Mr. Rich for permission, and he says, "No."

I said, "But my wife is at South Miami hospital."

He says, "I want you to think about it. You know your day's off is Thursday, we have to keep the floor covered. Who do you know personally who can go pick up your wife and child?"

I says, "Uncle Willard, Johannah's uncle."

He says, "So you'll call Uncle Willard."

So I called Uncle Willard and told him my dilemma, and he brought them home. So that was it.

What drives me? Oh, wow. I would say accomplishing something. I don't care how small it is, but I would like to carry it through to a successful ending. One other thing I taught all my kids : You do it now. You get a phone call, call back right now. Don't stack it up on your desk. If you do you're going to have 20 phone calls at the end of the day. And if you don't do it and put it off for the next day—you'll have 40. You have to do it now. Any task—no matter how small—do it now.

And I knock stuff out. I like to tackle a project and get it done. No time like the present.

But I love being successful. That term is relative. I do not need to appear prosperous. As you can see by my $90 watch I've had for 15 years and my Walmart pants and shirt, I don't enjoy spending money on myself but I do enjoy buying a building. And I enjoy doing a lot of things for other people.

But what motivates me? I want to be a success in everything I do every day.

But I'll tell you what I learned in high school that was very important: The day I graduated everybody was in the auditorium and we had a speaker that made my life easy. He got up to talk and you've got to remember, my dad didn't have a job, my mother was working for $40 a week at Winn-Dixie grocery store, I had one tooth missing in front and one chipped, I was sitting there and he was talking about the future and how you're should go out and accomplish things in your life. He said, "Some of you guys are going to be lawyers, some are going to be doctors, some are going to be accountants. That's not necessarily a success. I'll tell you what success is. Success is if you can achieve peace of mind and are happy."

And I'm thinking, damn, I can do that. I'm happy anyway. But I was concerned with my future. I was getting out of high school and jobs were hard to get.

He said, "Strive for peace of mind" and I've always remembered that. Because what is important? It's not how much money you've got in the bank, even though it gives you a great sense of security. And if you can help other people that's very rewarding. But if you can be happy with your life . . . and I'm extremely happy with my life. Really, really happy with my life and I think it shows when people meet me.

Why don't people ask me for money? That's a good question. A lot of people used to ask me for money. I said, "I don't loan money to anybody. No one. Why not? I'll tell you the story. I'll give you the Reader's Digest version.

Here's what happened: I'd been working hard since I was a kid and I saved up $5,000. It was in the bank a long, long time and I didn't touch it. Then my brother Gene came in one day and borrowed it. I didn't get my money back for 10 years. It's a long story. So word got out that unless you want to hear a long boring story, do not ask to borrow money from Don. Don't ask, you're not going to get it. And I don't loan money, but I do give it away to people who need it. But only if I see that need it and they don't ask for it.

Mount Rushmore and other ads:

After the infamous billboard sign, I was thinking of other things that would get attention to my ad for carpeting. There were so many ads in the Herald and the News back then. I thought it would be a good idea to run a picture of Mount Rushmore and pull one of the famous faces out and put my head in and say, "Don Bailey made history by taking inflation out of carpet prices." And that got a lot of attention.

The hole in the head was when I was with Expressway Carpets. A guy from the Herald came, and he was a good advertising man because he gave me good ideas. He said, "Don there's a guy in Detroit or Chicago and he's got a hole in the head. He became known almost overnight as the appliance dealer with a hole in his head. See him before you see anybody else." I thought it was great. So I ran it in the paper. My partner at the time said, "That's sickening, it makes me sick to my stomach. Don't ever do it again." And I didn't do it again even though it brought in a lot of customers.

But shortly after I left that partnerhip, he started running the ad with the hole in the head. His business cards had a hole in the head because he saw how many people came in because that was different. In New York, every ad he ran, the hole in the head.

Another fun ad was Mona Lisa. You know how she sits there with that smile? What I thought would be a good idea was Mona sitting but put in my face, and say, "You never know what kind of deal you're going to get at Don Bailey's." It was a real success.

But the naked carpet sign was the best ad by far.

The impact of the Depression:

It started when my dad was at the bottom and we lived in a little frame house in Georgia, no inside bathroom and no electricity. It was Christmas time and I was 4 and Jim maybe 2. And dad bought us for Christmas a peppermint stick, that was our gift. Well, Jim chomped his down, but I was thinking if I melt it, it would be bigger and I'd get more. So I asked my mom to put it in a frying pan. I watched it get destroyed.

My mother would always say, "Things are good now but they're not always going to be good." She said, "Things were good for Raliegh and I but then came the Depression. When that came we could hardly get anything to eat. We lost the business we had. The little bit we had in the bank, they closed the bank. There's a Depression coming, Don, and you better be ready for it. You better have money saved. You better have it in a place where you can get to it because if the bank closes you may not be able to get to it."

I always saved so I could make it through the next Depression. I don't think a week went by that she didn't talk about the Depression. And I talk to my son Don about it. Don is doing quite well financially and he made it on good investments on real estate. If you talk to his wife there's a Depression right now in their house because he's so conservative. Priscilla says, "The Depression is coming? I thought it came here several years ago."

Stealing a donkey:

Dad had saved a little bit of money from his Social Security check and mom's earnings and Jim and I, who still lived at home, contributed what we could. We needed a couch, and I'd seen this couch advertised in the paper. So we went over there and I took the ad with me and I said, "We want to buy this couch." Well, it was something like $39 and all the others were $100 to $150. He said, "Let me show you."

So he walked us through a bunch of nice couches and took us to the back and said, "This is it."

I said, "OK, we'll take it."

He said, "Well, well, uh, let me show you some other things we've got."

I said, "No, this is all the money we've got."

He says, "Is there any way I can show you . . . ?"

I said, "No."

He says, "I need you to sit on the couch. OK?"

It was like a day bed, then they had a board that they had wrapped in the upholstery with no cushion. You couldn't get comfortable in it. It was a lost leader they probably had been advertising for years and would get people in with the ad and switch them to something more expensive. But we bought it and they called some other salesmen over to look at us because they sold the coach.

Dad also found something to hang on the wall, and it had two little pieces of glass on it that you could put a figurine on. We got on the bus, went to Richard's department store and we found two figurines. They were $4 each. He says, "Don, we can't buy both, which one do you like?" "Well, I like the cat," or whatever it was. "I like the donkey."

He says, "I can only buy one."

So we bought the cat. We go home, he puts it on the thing. He goes in the kitchen and comes out and there's the donkey. I stole the donkey for my dad, and I have it to this day. I saved it for 60 years. It was my most prized possession because it was such a great memory with my dad, because I hardly ever got to see him. When he wasn't working, I was working.

One of the most humorous stories:

We had a store on 98th Street that wasn't doing too well because it was too close to our store on 148th so we decided to open one in Miramar. We couldn't find anything but there was this one building, where we are today. It wasn't for sale but I knew it was a good location. I walked in and said, "Listen, we're looking to buy a building and this suits are purpose. Are you interested in selling?"

He says, "You know, I was thinking about selling."

I said, "OK, how much is it?" And so forth. I said, "That's kind of a high figure, but if we can just put a little bit down, because we don't have much money, and if you'll hold the mortgage, I could buy it."

He said, "I can hold the mortgage."

I said, "Now I can't pay you interest. I can't afford it. But if you'll hold a five—or 10-year mortgage . . ."

So he says, "OK, you can buy it with no interest."

I was more or less kidding, when I said no interest.

So we set up the deal and we go to the lawyer, and the lawyer went to speak with the guy. They closed the door and we were waitiing in the outer office area. We were told, "Gentlemen wait out side, please. Have a seat."

So Jim had a seat. I went to the door and put my ear to the door. I heard the attorney say, "This is not ordinary. You don't have interest figured in here, you just have the sale price. What is the interest on the mortgage?"

The seller said, "I told him no interest."

The lawyer says, "You told him no interest? Ten years and no interest? You've got to get interest. We're going to get 10 percent interest. That's it."

"But I told him no interest."

And they argued back and forth. He said, "Well, I'm going to get you 10 percent interest."

I went back and sat down and grabbed a magazine. He said, "Come on back in guys." He says, "Everything is fine except the interest."

I said, "What interest?"

He said, "You have to pay interest wherever you go."

I said, "I pay interest to the bank. He's not a bank. If I was buying from a bank I'd pay the interest. Besides, we shook hands on it. Whatever happened to a gentleman's agreement? Whatever happened like in the old movies—it's a deal? Yes sir. Can we shake on it? He shook on it. He's not a bank."

And the seller says, "I'm not a bank, I don't need interest." I said, "Exactly. Thank you for living up to your word. I would have been very disappointed had you been lying to me."

And he said, "I've never lied to you. I'm no bank, no interest." He spoke in little broken English. I don't know where he was from, but he was a gentleman.

I make crazy offers and some times they accept it.

I have a dear friend named Peggy who went to school with Johannah. They had a baby shower for Peggy and no men were invited. I said, "That's not right, I've known her more than most of the women."

So I put on a wig and a dress and heels. I was married to Donna. Someone met me at the door and said, "I don't know this lady at the door but she's the ugliest woman I have ever seen."

Half the women recognized me and half didn't know me. I sat across from some of them and had my legs spread and no underwear on. A lady looks down at me and gasped, "Oh oh my God!" She calmed down and was whispering, "That woman has balls. They said that's Don Bailey."

I used to go 30 years ago to the Black Angus restaurant. They'd clog and dance, and I'd go on Friday night once a month.

They said if you ate everything on your plate, you'd get a balloon and a tin badge with a stamp on it that says Black Angus Sheriff. I asked the guy if I could have one. He said, "It's just for kids." I got one anyway and put it in my wallet.

For 10 years I could get into movies, boxing matches, I even took Ferdie Pacheco and Dr. Gordon to a UM game. I'd go to the end zone and see a security guard who was not too aware and say, "I'm the Black Angus sheriff" and I flipped it quickly."

One time I went to Gulfstream race track with six or eight people and I was treating. I said, "I need eight tickets" and flashed the Black Angus sheriff's badge, and she calls security. I said, "No I'm joking," She said. "You act like you're not joking." Donna made me throw the badge away. I was never refused except at Gulfstream.

Don toasting the good life.

Don flexes muscles in a holiday card.

6. CHILDREN AND WIVES

DON JUNIOR

I can't tell you how proud I am of Don because he's always been a great kid, never given me any trouble. He has always wanted to strive for excellence. In whatever he does, he dedicates himself. I have an article that appeared when he was a freshman in college. It was on the front page of the sports section in the Miami Herald written by Edwin Pope, and the title was, "Don Bailey keeps paddling ahead because of his dedication." Ed Pope talked about how dedicated he was. He was a starter as a freshman when the player who played center got injured. Anyone who has a son who played football has probably dreamed that their son would one day be a professional football player. Don Junior made that dream come true. For me what is so remarkable was how self-sufficient and self-motivated Don became coming from his parents' divorce. When his mother and I got a divorce, she moved Bobby and Jeannie, my two younger kids, to Vero Beach and she left Don with me. He was at an age that he could have gotten into all kinds of trouble. I never saw him because I would go to work early in the morning and I'd work late. He would get up, cook his own breakfast, fix his own dinner, wash his own clothes, iron his own clothes, do his homework, work out and practice football. He did everything on his own. Everything. I did nothing. I emotionally disappeared for a year, the first year, because I was really depressed. Thankfully, Don Junior had his good friend Al Hinson to drive and support him.

Then I met Donna, and Donna would come over and she was a good companion for both of us. She had a couple brothers around his age, so she was a buddy. She cooked for him.

Don Junior has never been a disappointment. And he still likes to aim for perfection and he tries to train employees in our flooring business to strive to be better. When he was coached by Howard Schnellenberger at University of Miami the motto was "strive for excellence". So no wonder, when he came in the business 25 years ago he quadrupled the sales in our flooring business. He listened to me while I was arranging carpet deals and real estate transactions and he learned. He also reads and listens to others in business and learns from them. Now he's 50 and running the business, has been running it for years. I'm here to help him, but he's the captain. He has achieved success in high school athletics, college football and professional football. Now he is an amazing businessman.

I'm so proud of him on the radio (560 WQAM) as the analyst for University of Miami football. I hardly miss any time he is on. I mostly listen in the car or we turn on the radio in the condo. Any time he is interviewed, he will call and I'll listen. I'm his biggest fan. I never miss the Canes coaches' show, and Donna and I pretty much camp out before the games wherever he is positioned at the stadium. During the games I'm uncomfortable with ear plugs, so Donna listens to Don Junior and relays all the information to everyone around us.

Not only is Don Junior excellent in sports and business, he has taken on the responsibility of our family. He takes care of his mother and worries and makes arrangements for everyone in our clan. He and his wife Priscilla are terrific together. She keeps him in great shape and keeps him healthy. He shows his love for everyone in our family and shares his valuable time with us. No son could make his father prouder.

BOBBY

Bobby is four years younger than Don Junior and went with his mother to Vero when he was around 11. I would go up every weekend when he played soccer. He won the award for the best soccer player. He was an outstanding football player. He scored three times in overtime as a halfback. He was voted the best running back in that tri-county area, up in Indian River County. His only hold back was he was undersized, 5-7, maybe 5-8, but the most fantastic athlete you've ever seen. The college coaches want bigger guys, but he was outstanding.

Now we see each other every week and he runs the real estate business. He runs it like a pro. He gives me all the information I need to guide him and for me to make decisions, but there's really not many decisions to make. Because he lets me know what's coming in, what's not coming in, what the taxes are, who's moving out, who's moving in. He's just done a terrific job and I'm very proud of him. He is quiet but always thinking and has a wonderful sense of humor. He has a wonderful wife, Josephine, and two great big dogs that I am afraid of. I am so blessed to have them in my life.

JEANNIE

I have a beautiful red-headed daughter. She is now a mother raising her 8-year-old boy, Adrian. Jeannie also moved to Vero with her mother after the divorce. I would write her every week and include one piece of gum. I missed having my children around and did my best to attend any important event in their lives. Jeannie had piano recitals. I also took her to Disney World at least once a year and later we would go to New York City for her birthdays. When she got married I was dancing with her and started to cry. She said, "Oh, Dad, don't be sad. I will still see you." And I replied, "I am crying because this reception cost me a fortune!"

I loved to tease her. Jeannie and her husband Roman live in Surfside, just over the bridge from me. Their son Adrian is such a terrific kid and I am enjoying being a grandpa. Recently I was back on the Miami Shores field watching Adrian play softball and remembering when my sons were there playing sports.

BRETT

My third wife, Donna, and I were not planning on any kids, but she got pregnant and it's such a joy. When Brett was born I couldn't believe it.

I was 55 years old at that time. And she is 18 years younger than me. I couldn't believe how happy I was. I cried when I saw him the first time. I really did. Being an older parent is totally different than having children when you are struggling and you do not know what kind of future you will have for your efforts. Brett got the benefits by having so much of my attention (whether he wanted it or not) and financially being able to enjoy whatever he desired . . . pretty much. He has got a great personality. He's funny, he's studious, he's going into his third year of law school. His love is music. He produces music, he plays three or four instruments.

He performed at Carnegie Hall with an orchestra. He's a disc jockey three nights a week over in South Beach even while he's in law school with all those hours of studying.

But he loves anything to do with music. Hopefully he will be able to incorporate law with music and use all his talents.

WIVES

Gloria and I went to high school together. I didn't know her then and I don't think she knew me. I met her maybe when I was 19 or 20 and we dated and we got married when I was almost 22. I wasn't ready to get married. First of all, I was a wild animal because my mother and father let my younger brother and I run wild. They were working all the time. We could stay up until 2 in the morning.

When I got married and after a couple of weeks I wanted to go out, because I was used to going out every night. And I just couldn't go home, and I continued to go out. And she continued to want me home. And I couldn't do it.

So, in a nutshell, she was a great wife, a great cook, a dedicated wife, and I was horrible. After we got our divorce, she didn't talk to me for 14 years, and when she referred to me it was Horrible Don. And when we finally started talking, we met at a party again, I got friendly with her husband, and she got friendly with my second wife, and we became very good friends.

But I always thought it was her fault that we got a divorce because she wouldn't let me go out at night and see women and drink and party.

I finally wrote a letter saying, "I just want to tell you Gloria what a wonderful wife you were and what a horrible husband I was." And also I had the Tiger Woods addiction, which sounds like a joke but is real. So when I was married to Gloria I was also engaged to marry my second wife, Johannah. And my fiancée didn't know I was married. And my wife didn't know I was engaged.

I'd been dating Johannah on and off, and finally gave her an engagement ring. And she came to my work place, I was working at Harry Rich, and it was about closing time and I saw her car lights flash. When I went outside she said, "There's a nasty rumor going around, Don, maybe you can clarify it."

I said, "What is it?"

She says, "I heard that you're married."

And I started stuttering and sputtering.

She said, "No, no, Don, that requires a yes or no answer."

And I said, "Yes."

She says, "Does your wife know about me?"

I said, "No, but I do intend to marry you."

And it was very hard to get a divorce from Gloria because she wanted to tame me, and it took awhile but I did. I sent her roses the day the divorce was final, a letter of apology and saying how bad I felt that I was such a bad guy, but I hoped she has a good life. And Johannah forgave me for being married and engaged to her, so we got married.

I write to Gloria, I talk to her every few months. She's a good friend and a wonderful human being.

Johannah was breathtakingly beautiful. She was a model. I fell in love with her looks the first night I saw her. We started dating when I was separated from Gloria and I was living with my mother and father. I used my dad's broken down car that had to be 25 years old.

When I dated her I had my good job at Harry Rich. At that time I was 25 and had just been named manager, from being a janitor and truck driver and salesman. I was making some good money, and she continued to work.

My first wife got my house and all the money except for $5,000 that I had saved since I was 12 bagging groceries, cutting yards, stealing hubcaps, radios, however I got it. Gloria always referred to it as the Holy Five because I wouldn't touch it. And I didn't tell Johannah about it. Johannah's first year working went to pay off the balance I owed Gloria. When we got married we first lived in a one-bedroom apartment off Biscayne Boulevard and 90th. We had one car. Some days she would take the bus downtown to work, some days I would walk to work, which was about eight to 10 blocks. About the time I got Gloria paid off, Johannah got pregnant after about two years of marriage.

I put the Holy Five down on a house in Miami Shores. I paid $16,000 for the two-bedroom house, $5,000 down. Johannah didn't work after baby Don was born. She was a wonderful mother to Don Junior, Bobby and Jeannie. She had the same problem that Gloria had, that I never stopped going out with other women. She'd catch me and forgive me, and I just couldn't stop. Eventually she wanted a divorce and I convinced her she was crazy to leave somebody like me. I mean, how could she? I talked her into going to a psychiatrist, so she went about every week for about a year. I don't know why a man with his education took a year to figure it out, but a year afterwards she came to me and she says, "You know Don, he thinks you're crazy. He thinks you're nuts and I'm OK. And what I want in this marriage is right."

I said, "Are you going to believe me or him?" She said, "I want you to talk to him." We go down there and he got to the point immediately. He says, "Don, she wants somebody who will come home most nights. More than that she wants somebody who doesn't cheat on her and run around with other women. And you've been doing that, and you were even married when you were engaged to her. How much more extreme can you get than that?"

He says, "So here's the question, and I need an honest answer. Don't beat around the bush. If she stays with you, can you come home at night and can you stop cheating?"

I guess I wanted to be funny or something but I said, "For how long?"

And he says, "For how long? For the rest of your life."

I said, "Look, what's today, Monday? I don't think I can make it til Friday. I swear to God I'll try."

He says, "Trying is not good enough. You've got to make up your mind that you can do it."

I says, "I can't do it. I can't do it."

And of course she left and moved into another house until the end of the school year and then she moved to Vero Beach and is there to this day. I still hold her in high regard and still send her a check every week. I've been doing that for 38 years. I could have stopped paying when my daughter Jeannie was 18; she's now 38. I'm going to continue to do it as long as I'm alive and she's alive.

Originally she got an attorney and he was a very tough attorney. When I saw the divorce agreement what they wanted I was enraged. I was going through what could have been a bankruptcy because I made a bad real estate investment. I didn't have much but I had my little carpet store, and with my brother maybe four buildings. When I saw the proposed settlement, I said, "You know what, I don't think this is enough. I think you should get it all. You're asking for 99 percent, just take it all. I'll tell you what's going to happen. As soon as the divorce is final, or maybe before, I'm going to California, Arizona, Las Vegas. You'll never hear from me again. I'll tell you what's going to happen to the carpet business. In 90 days there won't be a carpet business. The real estate? Give it a year. You won't know how to take care of the tenants. It is not as easy as you think. Now if you want to be fair with me, I'll go along with it. Just get rid of the attorney, then give me a list of your expenses and what you think is fair."

Well, she gave me a list and it was unfair. But it was unfair to her, not to me. And I told her, "Look, Johannah, you can't live on this. You want to send your kids to private school. Jeannie's only 3 years old, but eventually you want to send her to a good school. Bobby's in private school now. You've got living expenses, you've got gas, insurance. You can't do it. So what I'm going to do, I'm going to double what your asking for and that will give you a cushion for inflation."

And that's what I did.

Through the years we have remained on good terms. We celebrated family birthdays together and Christmas. We even went on a cruise and Johannah was in the same cabin with Donna and me. It was really best for the children to let bygones be bygones. She has found someone special in her life, and she always got along with Donna. Whenever I bring up paying Johannah all these years Donna, the most logical, reasonable and most clear thinking person I know, says, "Don this check is not hurting our lifestyle. She needs it, and give her whatever she needs." So we still send money. She will always have a special place in my heart because of the wonderful children we have together and the great friendship we once had.

Donna is the best thing that has ever happened to me in my entire life. According to Donna, "I saved the best for last." I introduce her as "My third and final wife"

The night I met Donna, I'd been divorced a little over a year, going out every night, I mean seven nights a week, going to the Bayshore Whale and Sail on 79th Street where all my friends went and partied. During that year I lost 50 pounds. I was a bit overweight. I was 225 and went down to 175 because in the mornings I'd stop by my mother's and have a piece of toast with melted cheese and a cup of coffee. No lunch and dinner was a quarter of a chicken. Maybe I'd go to the Bayshore and have some steak tidbits.

But the main thing, I was drinking every night to help me go to sleep. I really didn't sleep well for months. I came home one night and Don reminded me we had to go to a wedding at LaGorce Country Club. Our next door neighbor was getting married. I said, "Don, we are going to the wedding but I'm not going out any more. This is it. I'm exhausted, it's leading nowhere. This is the end of going out."

We go to LaGorce. At the reception we're drinking and, of course, I saw a lady that I was attracted to and I'd had a few drinks and I started thinking maybe I will start going out again.

Her name was Sue Federman. We were going out for drinks afterwards. I invited her, she readily accepted. She was 20 years younger than me. I was there with a couple of buddies and they were going to join us and then Donna walks by.

Now I didn't even see her face. I saw her shape and she took my breath away. And then I went down to her legs, and it's legs I've been searching for all my life. They're perfect. And I was thinking, what about the face? I didn't even notice her face? And I'm thinking, I don't care.

She stops at the dance floor, and she was watching people dance and was sipping on her drink. And I excused myself from Sue Federman and Tommy Jackson and Gail Purvis, who I was talking to at the time, and I went over and I said, "Listen, any future drinks you want, I want to pay for 'em."

And she said, "Well, they're free."

And I said, "Well, otherwise I wouldn't have offered."

And I chatted with her and I asked, "Would you like to dance?"

And she said, "Uh, sure."

So we started dancing, and she had a beautiful face too.

Here's what even made it nicer: She had a diamond watch with big, nice diamonds. She had a diamond ring and she had another sapphire ring.

Man, I married two women from the tenements, maybe I can get lucky this time. A lot of the women I had been dating were desperate for someone to take care of them. You were suspicious if they enjoyed you or the money you had. So someone rich seemed very interesting to me. What I didn't know, three generations of her family never had to work. The first generation made all the money. He was the mayor of Toledo, a big name. But the next generation didn't work, her grandfather was an artist and the next generation hardly worked. It got down to Donna and all they had was the diamond watch and the rings and two Tiffany lamps.

But I found out she was a treasure. We went for drinks afterward and started dating off and on. But I had a friend of mine, Ronnie Reicheck, who kept telling me, "She's young and she's beautiful. Why are you wasting your time? She's probably after your money."

And I said, "I don't care." But I was still pretty raw from the divorce and lacked trust.

And this was in my brain all the time: She doesn't care about you, she doesn't care about you. You need to do this: Go back to your wife.

I told Donna that I was interested in going back with my ex-wife and that I had three kids. And she said, "Don, if there's a chance for you to get back with your wife, you need to go and give it a try because of the kids." And she encouraged me for a couple of years. Johannah and I were talking about getting back together.

Then one night Johannah called after about two years and she said, "Don, I'd like to meet you in West Palm Beach, halfway between Miami and Vero Beach, and discuss getting back together." And there was a pause on the phone, and she says, "Don, did you hear what I said?"

And Donna was sitting 10 feet away with her legs crossed, mini skirt. And besides the physical features I'd found the most loving, understanding and most wonderful human being that I'd ever met in my life. So I looked at her, thought about Johannah and she said, "Don, do you want to meet?"

And I said, "You know, Johannah, no. We've talked for two years, and you change your mind and I can't do it anymore. I've found somebody that I really care about."

And she hung up on me.

So she may have been ready to go back and I wasn't. It was the best thing that ever happened to me. I continued to womanize and I continued to go out, and Donna understood that I was crazy. She said she knew what she was getting into when she met me. I didn't lie to her and she was patient. After awhile I didn't want to go out any more. I stopped going out. I think it was last Monday.

Just kidding, I don't do it any more. I stopped years ago. Really.

But for years she put up with a lot. I mean, after my first wife took everything, my second wife left me, we had a family. I was suspicious, I didn't know if I wanted to get married again.

She waited eight years for us to get married. Eight years. Patient all that time. And perfect in every way.

I remember our honeymoon; it was a Rhine River Cruise. Our first night onboard we were meeting other travelers and a couple said to us, "Sprechen Sie Deutch?"

"No."

"Tu parle Francais???"

"No."

So I figured they didn't speak English. Donna decided we should have champagne instead of the free wine and I went crazy like I always do when I have to waste money unnecessarily. And I said, "I don't give a s—if it is our honeymoon . . . drink the free crap." and the words got more graphic and Donna pointed to the couple and said, "Honey lets be civil around our new friends" and I said, "F—them, they don't even speak English . . . (I think I may have had a little jet lag).

So the next day we are walking through the cobblestone streets in Germany and we pass that same couple. We say "Good morning" and they say, "Hi Don and Donna. How is your day?" Come to find out they did speak English and they just thought we looked foreign. We had to dine with them for seven days and toward the end of the trip they actually started liking us.

So here we are 36 years later. And every morning I wake up happy as I can be because she's there next to me.

We were together about 13 years and she got pregnant and we had Brett. Donna became the best mother ever. She has been devoted to both Brett and me and we both know how fortunate we are.

She's my best friend, absolutely, by far. It's not that she doesn't tick me off now and then, when she's more logical than I am. She is the best person I ever met in my life.

Don with his three wives (from left) Gloria, the first;
Donna, third and final; and Johannah, second.

Family birthday at Benihana's (from left) Roman, Adrian and
Jeanne Sparkacz, Josey and Bob Bailey, Don and Donna.

Family trip to New York (from left) Donna,
Adrian, Roman, Josey, Jeanne, Bob and Don.

Don's 78th birthday dinner (from left) Josey,
Bob, Brett, Don, Don Junior and Priscilla.

7. THE BAILEY FAMILY

DON BAILEY, JUNIOR

In answering the question of what is it like to be Don Bailey's son, there are a couple of versions, and both of them are great.

The son of the man on the billboard has always gotten the response: "Is that you on that billboard?"

"No, that's my father."

"Wow, that's your dad?"

In '72, '73, I'm 10, 11 years old. The billboard was way ahead of its time.

It's always been exciting to be his son. I've always been proud to be his son.

The other side is, I've had the best teacher forever. Forever.

When it comes to business, we don't always agree but he's always a good sounding board. The thing he did, as far as being a son and a family, I think the best thing that happened to me was he saw Harry Rich and his son not get along and lose the biggest name in the industry. It would be like me not being in business with him and him dying and the name dies. He saw that happened at Harry Rich.

As a son and a father in business together, he's allowed me to make mistakes and he's allowed me to grow.

It's fun.

Since I was 14 years old, it was he and I. There's always been mutual respect. And there's been a line there. I remember vividly hearing him say, "Hey, I'm not one of your freaking friends at school. I'm your father."

When stuff would get out of hand and you're growing up and you're a teenager, he rarely would come down on you. He's not a big disciplinarian. It's more you don't want to hurt him.

He's not "You be in at 8 or you're grounded." He didn't do that. My mom kind of was the enforcer on that side of it. But you never wanted to hurt him, that's why you toed the line. He didn't set a lot of boundaries, but he never wanted you to be hurtful to people. He always had people's feelings in mind.

I came home way too late many nights in my early teens. Or didn't come home. He didn't say a whole lot about that.

But he was a big attitude guy. You've got to have the right attitude, you've got to be understanding of mankind. He's big on that. There are two sides to the story, always.

It's crazy because I had him as a father but also as the best friend. It's that simple.

And fortunately, probably, I didn't need the father as much. And I mean that in a good way. He was a very good father.

If I need my father—we're so used to being friends and business associates—I say, "Hey, I need my dad for a minute." Kind of change gears.

And he was always there.

He worked. He was gone in the morning and came home. It wasn't a 4 o'clock in the afternoon deal.

But I remember to this day I was in 75-pound football and it was a 12 o'clock kickoff or something. And I remember we were getting ready to play, and I was good back then when I was a little peewee. I was good. I remember having my hand on the line and I was playing defense at the time, and I kept waiting for my dad. And I remember looking to the sideline and seeing his white pants, and I knew it was time to play.

He would be at everything that was important. Every single time.

Whether it was for me or my brother. If it was a younger brother playing sports, he was there every single time. My sister's piano recital—he had to drive two and a half hours and turn around and drive home? He was there.

That's why to this day, I go to dinner with him once a week, at least. And we walk once a week, at least, in the morning. Just he and I. I pick him up at 7, and he never says no. Think about that.

I've never called him and he's never been down on the phone. Ever. He's never too busy to take my call. Never. Never. Never.

I think his whole life was his kids. His business too. He worked for his kids. He worked for himself, but he worked for the joy of it.

I don't know if anybody's got a father that was more dedicated to his kids, but he and his sons? Nothing better. Nothing better.

Best teacher in the world. And let me tell you, he won't stop teaching you. He will just pound you and grind you in a great way. Prove it to you, or you're going to have to prove you're right.

He and I get into some intense conversations with business. I'm more intense than he is, but he's a hard sale. You've got to convince him, which is what you want.

I made many mistakes. And he wouldn't beat you up on a mistake. That's the great thing about him.

I remember one time he told me to sell somebody this product, this category of product, and I sold them the other category of product and he just shook it off. And after the person left, he said, "This is why I told you to do this. And this is why you shouldn't have done this." And explained it and wrote it down.

I mean, he spends his life giving directions to you like you were a fifth- or sixth-grader, and not in a condescending way. Not like he's talking to a child.

Somebody taught him communication is the key. If you write something, write like you're writing to a third grader, or a fifth grader. And that's how he is. And he explained it and he didn't grind on it, he didn't embarrass you on it. And he let it go.

I didn't make mistakes again and again and again. Now if you make mistakes again and again and again, he gets tired of that. He doesn't have a lot of patience for attitude or stupidity or laziness.

His thing growing up was: "I punish according to attitude." He meant that.

He's never had an attitude. He's 78 years old. I pick up the phone, and I try to give him a heads up before we walk, and he's not a great sleeper. He might have gotten two hours sleep.

Pop, you feel like walking?

"How long til you'll be here?"

Give me 10 minutes.

"Meet you downstairs."

One of the greatest things was, he used to live four houses away. We see each other at work and it's all business. But I like to have him as my dad during the week, too.

He's my best friend. Aside from Priscilla, he's my most trusted friend.

Childhood memories:

As a kid I'd go in the bathroom with him and he would be shaving and he'd give me shaving cream and I'd shave with a comb. And one time he got out of the shower, his hair was wet and he combed it to the sides and then he took a piece and combed it right down the middle. He said, "This is the new style. This is how people are wearing it now, I want you to know that." So there's a picture of he and I like that.

And the next morning I get ready to go to kindergarten and he combs his hair with that one piece coming down the middle. And I comb mine like that. He drove me to school and said, "Have a nice day." I got out of the car, and I remember people saying something to me. And I remember saying, "Hey, my dad wears his hair like that."

You know how kids are. I looked like the biggest idiot in the world. He said the minute I got out of the car he pulled his comb out and combed his hair over. And he said he just laughed all the way to work, that he pulled that off.

I think I got even with him a couple of times, because—this is God's truth—I'll tell you exactly where it was: It was on 96th Street and NE 6th Avenue. I was 5, and he's driving me to the same kindergarten and he says, "What do you have in the box?"

I said, "It's for school."

"Well, what do you have in the box?"

I said, "Here, you want to see?"

He said, "Sure."

And I open the box and a frog jumps out and jumps on him and onto the window. We're at a red light. He jumps out of the car hollering at the top of his lungs.

In his mind it was a poisonous toad that was going for his eyes. Anything he hated was going for his eyes. He finally had to jump back in.

One time he was driving me to kindergarten or first grade and he says, "Damn I'm running out of gas and I don't understand it."

I told him, "You can't be running out of gas, daddy?

"Why is that?"

"Because I filled it up last night."

"How did you fill it up?"

"While I washed the car I filled it up with water."

"You little SOB."

We ended up running out of gas right on 6th Avenue.

Him taking me to school, we had some adventures.

One time, it was the best fun I ever had in my life. We lived in San Souci, and they were building a house and we all piled in a van. He owned an old used van, $100 van.

We're piling in and he's dropping us off at school. And he gets in the van and grabs the steering wheel and dog crap was on the steering wheel. And it came through on his hands.

Nobody knows where it came from. My brother and I laughed so hard, I cried. For some reason I think it was on one of our shoes, but nobody ever admitted it.

He was there at every football game, every game, everything that was important.

One of the best things he did for me was he sent me to Hialeah-Miami Lakes High School. I was having trouble in ninth grade at Curley and I didn't fit in. It was the only year I didn't play sports. He sent me out there to HML to be with coach Joe Brodsky and Vinny Hines. And I ended up having a great career there. It wasn't easy. I couldn't have lived any farther away from there at the time.

He sent Al Hinson to pick me up and it was a good experience. But dad was there every game, junior varsity. And college he was there. In the pros he would go as much as he could go. He's always there, to this day, all the kids. Always there.

As a kid every morning I would wake up, I would crawl out of my crib or get out of my bed and would go into his room and I would say, "Daddy, tell me about the fox." That's why you see foxes around our house. And he would tell me a story about the farmer and the fox, how the fox would get in the hen house and the farmer would shoot him or scare him away. But now as I've gotten older I realize that my dad was 32, 35, 38. He could have been out partying the night before. I'm positive he had been working his ass off, and he needed his sleep as well. He wasn't coming home and taking naps. He wasn't taking a day off. He worked as hard as he could and played as hard as he could. He played it at both ends for many years and was always able to tell the story about the fox. And I don't know how many dads would not say. "Son, go back to sleep, hush up, dad's tired." He'd tell me the same story again and again and again.

But that's him and it's no different today. I'll call him tomorrow morning at 7 o'clock and I'll say, "Dad, let's go for a walk," and he'll say, "OK." He may not have slept a wink. "I'll be ready in 10 minutes." And he'll have a story for me. It may not be about the fox. I guess he's never stopped telling that story, it's just the person or the thing has changed.

I remember National Signing Day. Joe Brodsky and Arnie Romero were recruiting me for the University of Miami, and I thought that's where I was kind of going. But they all stayed out of it. My dad stayed out of it. They let the process go. Florida State and Florida were recruiting me, and this and that. Coach Brodsky's son Larry was down there, and I kind of thought that's where I was going, in the back of my mind. I just said, "That's it."

It was National Signing Day and I was in HML in coach Mike Uspensky's office. They had called me down, and the coach from Auburn says, "Hey, we're flying down tonight and we want to sign you to Auburn."

I don't know how it worked that I hadn't signed yet. I don't know if the guys hadn't come for the scholarship yet. I remember pressing that hold button on the phone and calling my dad. I go, "Dad, a guy is on the phone from Auburn and he says he's coming down and he wants me to sign a scholarship tonight."

And he says, "Don, tell that man that you're going to the University of Miami, because who the hell can we sell a rug to in Auburn, Alabama." And I says, "OK." That was it. That's how he thought about it.

And I think he honestly thought I was going into the business anyway. I'm sure he hoped it, I don't know if he knew it but I'm sure he hoped it.

I talk to him every single day. Like I'll go away for 10 days, I won't call in because I need a break. We'll go right to business. But every day that he's in town and I'm in town, I talk to him every day. Not just work talk, but on my way home. I usually call him on my way home.

"You home yet?"

He talks me home. Every day.

He's always got the best attitude in the world. And what he's done for people, it never stops. He sees the person first and has a heart for the underdog, always. Really. He really does.

Why did I decide to go into the family business? It kind of evolved. When I was released the last time in the NFL from the Colts, I kind of realized I had done everything humanly possible to play professional football and I just wasn't able to catch on like I thought I would have. And I came home and took a week off. I remember that (Don Bailey Carpet) is where I went. I'd been going there since I was a kid. And how could it be bad? My dad's there.

How bad a deal could that be?

You get to go to work with your dad. You get to go to work with Al Hinson, who would walk me home from first grade? Where else do you go?

I think I stayed in it because I love Miami. I think I stayed in it because I love being there, I love who I'm with.

It's not an easy job. It's very challenging.

I look back, and Priscilla and I had a conversation, I was going to go into coaching. There was a crossroads for me. I was drawn back to football. And I just couldn't get away from it. The crossroads was the coaching and the flooring.

And that's how the radio evolved, because I was able to get my fix of football and be around it in a big way and have feelings about it. Help the kids and be around those people. I'd get my fix that way.

So I was able to get the best of both worlds because, look, if I'm going to get into coaching we're going to bounce all over the place. I don't want to leave. I love Miami. I've lived my whole life within a couple miles of this.

I had no set career plan. How could it be a bad day if I get to go to work with my dad and Al Hinson? And that hasn't changed. It's still a great team to be on.

I really wanted to do this. When I think about it, and I'm sincere, I get to go to work with my dad, who's my best friend, I get to build something with him, I get to work through problems with him, I get to face all the challenges and learn everything he knows and be with one of my favorite people on earth every single day. And having Al there, who walked me home when I was in the first and second grade, so how do you not do that? How do you not be with the people you love and appreciate the most?

Plus I enjoy it.

My first reaction to the billboard: See, my dad has never shocked me. My dad has been that dad my whole life. I remember the picture that they took that my uncle painted off of, that they shot in our living room. And I remember seeing the painting. I don't remember a shock of seeing it. But I remember the people asking, "Is that your dad? Is that your dad on the billboard? Is your dad crazy? What's wrong with your dad? Are you Don Bailey?" That's what you remember.

That's like asking a Ford what is it like to be a Ford.

That billboard is our trademark, it's his trademark. Once again you go back to the shock treatment he'll give people, whether it's what he'll say, or what he'll do or what he's done.

My mom was on one billboard. I remember going down to the Keys (and thinking): Oh, there's dad. There's mom. You remember that.

It still doesn't shock me. That's him.

It's a great marketing tool. I was out recently at a client's. "Are you . . . ?" Right away the billboard. "I remember on Okeechobee Road you had a billboard. Is that you?"

"No, that's my pops."

"Your dad, is he crazy?"

"Yeah, a little bit. Every day. Thank God."

Him and the Coppertone girl. And he's proud of it, man. It's right up his alley.

And you know what? It's turned out to be a part of Miami, a part of South Florida. People are proud of it. People who don't know the story are proud of it. That's our crazy Don Bailey. It's a part of our community.

I get asked all the time, "When are you going to be there?"

Never. Never.

It will always be his. It's a part of our fabric of South Florida.

Just talk about it, that's all that matters.

But that's all the icing. The story behind it is the cake with him. How he is with people. How he is with business. There isn't anybody who wouldn't do a deal with him again. And that's a compliment.

He'll always be very fair.

The thing about him, he keeps learning. We wake up dumb and poor every day. We try to learn something and we try to earn something every day. We really do.

We've always learned from other people. Always. And always think that the Depression is right around the corner. Which it has been these last few years.

He doesn't live like millionaire. Tha's not him. He's still a truck driver. I think he cares more about the truck driver than the millionaire.

The millionaire is the game that he plays. The person that he is is the truck driver. The business. Now believe me, he wants nice stuff. He's going to provide, but he's not a flashy guy. He doesn't even change clothes. Wears the same pants five days in a row.

You go on a trip and he'll take a toothbrush for three days. I'm not kidding. He'll walk out of a restaurant if he thinks it's overpriced.

He never forgot making $50 a week. He's always known the value of a dollar. He's not gonna get ripped off, he's not gonna rip somebody off. He's doesn't live that way; I don't live that way.

I'd still be driving a 12-year-old truck if one of our drivers didn't total it. And he drives the standard Ford F-150. That's just what he does, he's a humble man.

He's not jewelry and Rolexes and this and that. But his finances allow him to do whatever he wants when he wants to. But what you see is really what he is.

He's not a flashy guy. He's got flashy stories, flashy smile. He's not worried about impressing anybody in that respect. He's humble.

Open house: He opened our home, wherever I was, to all of my friends and my teammates. When I was at UM, come Thanksgiving, whoever wanted to come to my house, and I don't mean just my roommates.

Everybody came. Whoever was here. I remember having Keith Griffin and Speedy Neal, Tony Fitzpatrick and myself, Priscilla I believe was there at the time. We'd have Thanksgiving dinner. He'd take us out to dinner. Everybody was always welcome, it didn't matter where they were from, it didn't matter what position they played, it didn't matter what level they were. It was everybody's always welcome. He's had the greatest open-door policy for friends of mine that you could have.

The hurricane came in 1979. I don't remember the name of it—whatever hurricane scare my freshman year at UM. It was Ed Hudak and myself and five or six players came to our apartment. We had to leave campus. So we loaded up the car and we're going to Baileys. Coach Howard Schnellenberger said we've got to get off campus, they're evacuating campus, take how many you can.

And that's what he did. He always makes everybody feel welcome. He's got the greatest ability to make people feel that they're the most important person in the world, and he means it. And he wants them to feel that way.

My high school friends, my college buddies. And to this day, everybody within 30 seconds or a minute of a conversation, whether it's all the guys I played football with, I'm talking to Clem Barbarino, who's in Pittsburgh: "How's your dad? Tell your dad I said hello." And Tony Fitzpatrick: "Donny, how's pops? Tell him I was asking about him."

Today I talked to a guy at the mill in Georgia, he's my age but we've gone out to dinner with him, Kelly McClain, at Mohawk Industries. I called him and I'm talking about business and I'm coming up there, I'm on the phone one minute: "How's your daddy doing?"

And they seriously want to know. That's the kind of impression he makes on them. And he's always done that. And it's not just my friends, it's everybody he meets every day.

When I think of my dad and the kind of person he is, he's always going to make everybody feel like they're the most important person in the world.

For the last five, six or seven years, we go to Vermont Fourth of July weekend. I'm going. It's probably the best four- or five-day period that we have as a father and son the whole year. We're away from everything and everybody's totally decompressed. And it's my favorite four or five days of the year.

If I go to Alaska for two weeks or biking in California for 10 days, I'd trade all of the trips for those four or five days. It's probably the only period of time where we really turn it off. Here in Miami it's always up, the hustle, the deal, and it never turns off. It slows down and we have moments. But that is total father-son, father-daughter-in-law, and Donna. It's the best.

We do something together every single day. He's 78 years old and will go canoeing. He tells Donna the whole time how to steer. And moans and groans. "Turn right!. Watch out!"

And we torment him, too, and he knows it. It's a good deal. We all go to the Fourth of July parade, hometown, and fireworks display. If he lives to be 100—and he can get there—we'll be there come hell or high water.

Beause it's beautiful.

A beautiful time.

A CONVERSATION WITH PRISCILLA AND DON JUNIOR

PRISCILLA: What is it like being the daughter-in-law of Don Bailey? What is it like when they find out you're Don Bailey's daughter-in-law?

They ask about the sign. I say, "It's my father-in-law, not my husband. It's Don Senior, not Don Junior."

Then they laugh and they say when was the last time they saw it or where they first saw it.

I don't know what it's like to be his daughter-in-law because I've never had another father-in-law. I'm not sure how it's supposed to be. It's different than anybody I know. He is unique.

Because I'm from a more traditional family, regular parents, sister and brother and all that, when I first met him I was a little bit shocked, to say the least, with some of the shenanigans that went on.

It was fun, it was different. I stayed at Don Junior's house a lot. We went out to dinner a lot with them on Sunday nights. You never knew what he was going to say or what he was going to do. Like when my dad had to meet him, I was worried about that because my dad was a guy that was in the Navy, was a fireman, he was a little bit older than Don Senior. He never cussed in front of us, never told raunchy stories, never crossed the line. My dad was not a strict father, a fun father, but not like Don Senior.

It was scary when he first had to meet Don Senior. I was worried about what Don Senior was going to say. The whole time I was on edge worried about when he had to meet my sister, my brother. I was worried about what he was going to do or say.

Now I'm used to him. And my sister and my brother-in-law enjoy him. My brother is a little bit older, a lot older than I am, and very traditional, very straight laced. And I think he is not sure how to take Don Senior still. I don't think he gets it, I don't think he understands the whole thing.

My friends love him when they meet him. He can be very charming and interesting and fun.

I only see that when it's just Don and myself and him out for an evening. He can be very charming. He's still amusing but he's not on.

And I like that side of him more than the other side. I appreciate that side more, I can relate more to that side than the crazy, goofy side.

It's different, very different.

I didn't grow up here, I grew up in New York. I didn't see the billboard or know anything about Don Bailey Carpets. Actually I think our first dorm room at UM we bought Don Bailey Carpet but we didn't know it.

Somebody said, "Where do you buy carpet for the dorm room?" And my roommate and I went up and bought it. But they didn't have sign on the side of the building or anything then, it was on the other side.

My first reaction? I liked it, I thought it was funny, I thought it was interesting, the naked carpet man. Yeah, I liked it. I didn't think it was so bad. I knew the City of Miramar was having problems with it, but I didn't think there was anything bad about it. I thought it was clever.

Favorite memories: He took me on a cruise every Christmas for about 10 years, the whole family. That was nice; I'd never been on a cruise before.

Johannah, the second wife, and Donna, and Don and Jeanne and Bobby and Dondi and myself and Bobby was married briefly there, too, and Becky came with us. All in one cabin. No, I'm kidding. I think we had two cabins.

I remember driving up to Vero Beach after I'd known Dondi for about a month. He said, "We're going with my dad and Donna."

"Where are we going? We're going to Vero Beach? Well, I thought your mother lived there."

"She does. We're going to stay with her."

"Well, where's your dad and Donna staying?"

"Well, they're staying with her too."

"We're all staying with your mother?"

"Yeah."

And I thought that was like the weirdest thing. But it wasn't. We got up there, and everybody got along. Johannah moved out of her bedroom and gave Donna and Don Senior her master bedroom. I guess she slept with Jeanne. That was different. It was all different. I had never been around stuff like that. It was not what I was brought up with.

He was always fun loving. I never heard him say anything mean or negative. Always happy. He's never sad.

He does more than anybody I know. Like they'll be on a vacation and come home on a Sunday and I'll say to Don, "Isn't your dad coming home from wherever?" And he'll say, "Yeah I think he's coming home this morning."

And he'll call him at noon and they're already out at the movies or he's at work or they're out shopping, You'd think they'd come home and put their clothes in the laundry, just kind of hang at home. He's never home. He's always out, always wanting to do something.

We'll go out to dinner and Don and I will be like, "Well it's 10 o'clock and we're going home." And he'll go, "You know, there's a club down the street that has music and blah, blah, blah." Don and I go, "We'll see you, we're tired. He never stops."

He took us to New York one time and I don't think we ever took a cab. We walked the whole time. That was fun. He loves to walk.

Mr. Energy.

He always has energy for everything.

DON JUNIOR: He appreciates Priscilla. And I can tell you from the other side of it, he respects her academic accomplishments and her volunteer work, Operation Smile. He really respects that and appreciates it. And I know he's proud of that a lot.

PRISCILLA: It's a volunteer organization based out of Norfolk, Virginia, and we go internationally and we fix clef lips. It's great, it's a good group. The founder is a plastic surgeon and his wife is a nurse. And they went to the Philippines and noticed a lot of kids have clef lips and palettes and they didn't understand why. And they did some research and said, "We've got to fix this." So they started going to the Philippines and the whole purpose is: we'll fix 250 kids in a week. And their purpose is to teach the people of that country about volunteering and to do it on their own. We're not going there just to do it. It's taken off, and they do just incredible stuff.

There are probably about two or three missions going on every week. They've fixed I don't know how many thousands and thousands of children.

I knew the story of the truck driver's helper to being successful, I didn't know to being millionaire because the way he lives you wouldn't know he's a millionaire. I just know he's comfortable.

It's pretty amazing to go from where he started to where he is now and do whatever he wants to do. But they don't fly first class, he doesn't wear fancy clothes. He's very simple in his tastes and stuff, but he'll do whatever he wants to do.

I'll say, "Gosh I can't believe he's doing that." And then he'll be worried about spending a dollar for a cup of coffee. He'll spend whatever for someone else, he'll spend an incredible amount of money. And then we'll be out to dinner and he'll be looking at the menu and saying, "Oh, wow."

Or a lot of times you go out to dinner with him and he doesn't order and eats what everyone else doesn't eat. He doesn't order a meal but stares the whole time while you're eating and you're thinking, "Oh, I guess I've had enough of this, pass it down." He won't order a meal because he wants to save the $10 for the meal. And you hear the day before he bought whatever for $1,000 for someone else.

Or he was worried when we went to Joe's Stone Crab, it was a business thing. And Donna and I were at the bar, we each had a glass of wine and when the check came the two of us turned because we didn't have purses, of course, and he couldn't have gotten away fast enough. Just to not pay for our bar tab. He scurried away. We looked at each other. She said, "Do you have money?" I said, "No." She said, "I don't either."

We had to get Dondi to get our bar bill. He picks and chooses when he's going to be magnanimous and act like he has money. It's not all the time.

DON JUNIOR: He could be rich man, poor man, within in hour. It could be 15 minutes.

PRISCILLA: Yeah, it's the audience. It's true. If it's just you and me and we're out, he's not touching the bill. But if my girlfriend's come, "Oh, sit down, have a drink, I'm buying."

DON JUNIOR: I'm telling you from Day One memory, he will stare at your plate. "Are you done yet?" He'll eat off your plate. He's the guy that would go and open a box of candy at my grandmother's and take a bite and put the other piece back, the other half.

PRISCILLA: Or if I've baked a cake, I'll come home and I'll know Don Senior was there because the icing is missing off the top of the cake. He won't cut a piece, he'll scrape the top of the icing off.

DON JUNIOR: On the other hand, he used to make us hand him his water holding the glass at the bottom because he didn't want our hands near the top because of the germs.

PRISCILLA: He's worried about germs. He's germaphobic.

DON JUNIOR: We all go to Joe's Stone Crab for my mother's birthday or Priscilla's or whatever it is. He will not order. If he does, he'll order the fried oysters, which are the least expensive thing on the menu in seafood. And then he will eat off everybody's plate.

When we would go to Mike Gordon's (restaurant) he would highly recommend the fish sandwich. It's the best in town, which was also the least expensive thing in town. Do you realize he will wear the same pair of pants for a week?

PRISCILLA: We're on a cruise, he'll wear the same pants all week.

DON JUNIOR: He'll go away for three days and take a toothbrush. That's it. To New York City. And he'll maybe bring a jacket. Not a suit jacket, a jacket jacket. That's it. No socks, no underwear. That outfit and that's it. Go to bed at night, take his pants off, lay his shirt down, hang 'em up, go to sleep, get up, put 'em back on.

PRISCILLA: Does he shop for clothes? He wore that little green robe forever.

DON JUNIOR: But he's one of the most organized people you'll ever know. He used to keep a little man on his dresser and called him the Little Man. He still has it. He comes home, his keys are in front of the Little Man, his change is there. Everything is exactly in its place. Everything.

PRISCILLA: And you know he is not happy with you if you get a note with a black flair pen on a white piece of paper. If he's not happy with something, you get a note. He still does that.

DON JUNIOR: That's how he reprimands you. I got in trouble a couple of times. I came home from college one time, I had a little situation and he heard about it, I walked into my bathroom and there was a note taped to the mirror on the medicine chest. That's how he would handle it.

PRISCILLA: He won't say anything but he'll write you that note.

DON JUNIOR: But he'll say a lot in that note. We've all gotten notes.

PRISCILLA: I've saved all my notes.

DON JUNIOR: But he'll write beautiful notes, too. And he'll write a nice card as well. I think it's easier for him to reprimand by note than by face to face.

He would have been an unbelievable lawyer. He could have argued points to death. If he had picked a career that would be a professional deal, it would be law. He'd be part corporate, part ambulance chaser, part advocate. And he could argue one side as well as the other, I'm sure. I see that in him.

And he's unbelievable with numbers and finance. He gets it. He has his own way but it's a good school.

PRISCILLA: He's always thinking. I don't think he takes time off.

DON JUNIOR: We're both that way. We have to leave town to rest.

PRISCILLA: He's always thinking. He'll be sitting there and you'll be watching him and he'll say, "You know what? If we sell that building and move this over here . . ." We'll be watching the Super Bowl and he'll be thinking about that. Always thinking.

DON JUNIOR: He really respects the battle that (former UM player and coach) Randy Shannon has fought from his beginning to where he is. There's a huge amount of respect for Randy's story. It's not being head coach, or that he was head coach. That impressed him the least. What impressed him the most was what he battled through. He identifies a lot with that. That's why he's a Randy Shannon fan. He really respects him. There were a lot of battles he identified with.

ROBERT (BOB) BAILEY

The main way my dad has been special in my life: He has taught me to be a person, and most importantly how to be a good business person. I think that's where I learned the most.

And he's always there to help you out if you need something. If there's ever a problem about anything, you can call him.

There's nothing hiding from him. He's been through it all several times, so any problem I've encountered in my life, he's been through it before. He's been able to give me a lot of guidance. Just pretty much anything you'd expect a great dad to do.

He's always been there through tough times, through good times. Someone you can always count on and depend on. He doesn't really judge you, he tries to help you along and make you a better adult.

I take care of all the real estate for the family business, so I talk to him usually two or three times a day, some times even more. He's been doing the real estate for 40 years, so he's got so much experience and knowledge in dealing with people. Anything that has come up he's seen it before, he's had to deal with it before. He's a great teacher and explains everything in a way that's very easy so you understand. There's no gray area with him.

I work out of my house in Fort Lauderdale. When I got out of college, the University of Florida, I went to work for him in the carpet store. I was doing that for about 20 years. And then I left maybe six or eight years ago and I worked at a commercial recording studio for about three years.

And at that time he needed someone to run the real estate because it had started to grow. And I was looking for something, so it was a perfect fit. I'd been with him all these years when he had done real estate and stayed involved in it. The timing worked out good where I was able to come in and take over and run everything.

Special memories: After sixth grade, when mom and him got divorced, I moved up to Vero Beach with my mom and my sister. Every summer I'd come down and spend the summer with him.

I know the first summer we went on vacation. He took me to Japan and Thailand and the whole Orient for two weeks. Just me and my dad and Donna. I must have been about 13 or 14. We had just a fantastic time. The following year we went to Africa for a safari for two weeks, my dad and Donna.

He asked me where I wanted to go and the first one was the Orient and the next year I wanted to go to Africa. So he enabled me to go to two places I probably never would have gone to without his help. I traveled with him a lot when I was young.

I always enjoyed the traveling. He exposed me to so many different cultures and different things that you would never learn without traveling. You know, the way they do things in Africa is so much different. And the Orient was so much different. Just very interesting seeing the different cultures and just everything about them. It shows you there's a lot more to the world than what you see every day.

In Japan we went on an organized tour for a week, then Bangkok, the outskirts of Thailand, and we went to Hong Kong. It was a guided tour but it was very interesting.

In Africa we went to Kenya for two weeks on a picture taking safari. We saw everything, from lions to elephants. One night we had a herd of zebra come through our camp. Birds, cheetahs, pretty much anything you could imagine. Hippopotamus. We got pretty close because we were in vans out in the brush. It was never dangerous; we never got too close.

He enjoyed it. Vacation to him was getting away and spending time not worrying about his business.

I was 12 when I moved to Vero. It was a tough age. My mom and dad were always on friendly terms. There was never a problem. So as a 12-year-old I didn't see any of the fighting or any of that stuff. And I talked with him a lot and saw him in summers. It was good because I got all his attention during the summer, where if I was with him all the time I probably wouldn't have gotten that.

I know when I was in high school he'd drive up and see me play football or soccer games. He'd make the drive up to Palm Beach or Vero, so I'd see him during the school year, too. Spring break I'd come down and see him.

I probably didn't know it at the time because I was 12, it still was kind of a happy family. Never any fighting. I don't remember any of that.

What is it like being son of the naked carpet man? Wherever you'd go there would always be a story. Someone would find out who you are. "Oh, your dad . . ." and they'd have a story about something they did together or back in the day this or that.

Everyone that has met him has a great story that they've done something with him. He's affected a lot of people's lives, almost all for the positive. Everyone has a story and loves talking to him.

As for the billboard, I think I was just used to it because when he did it I must have been 10, before I went to Vero. It's just something that's always been there. I don't know anything else, it's just always been around.

I also played baseball and lacrosse all through junior high and high school. Nothing in college. A lot of the away games he and Donna would drive up to Boca Raton or Palm Beach to see me play football or my soccer games. A few times they'd come up to Vero and stay for the weekend if I had a soccer game or something. Always very supportive. If we'd travel to Boca or Palm Beach, a lot of times he'd be the only parent there. He was always very good about that.

In football I played running back, in soccer I was a winger, same thing in lacrosse. Baseball I was in the outfield.

Some times we'd go on charter fishing trips, usually out of Haulover before I moved to Vero. Mostly it was time to get away and for us to get together.

As for the real estate business, he and his brother bought a duplex and then bought something else and it snowballed from there. As a kid I remember we'd drive around and if we had to go somewhere, if he was taking us to the zoo, he'd always stop off and look at some real estate property on the way. It's something he's always done.

Do I have Don Bailey carpet in my home? Oh yeah, have to have that. It comes with the territory.

JEANNIE STERKACZ

Being Don Bailey's daughter can be described as interesting, great, never a dull moment, going on lots of trips.

My favorite time with dad was on my birthday when we'd go to New York City for 11 years. That was my favorite time with him. He'd still be in the work mode but in New York he was completely there and enjoyed himself. They were the best trips. Me and Don and Donna. Friday to Sunday night.

We did everything there—plays, walked a lot. He doesn't like taking cabs, dresses way he dresses.

One time we were walking down the street and it was real windy and we went in to Macy's to get out of the wind and a lady came out of Macy's and tried to put money in his coffee cup because of the way he was dressed—jeans with a hole in it. After that he put his hand over his coffee cup.

My parents divorced when I was 3. I was in Vero Beach.

He came up to see me, Dondi and Bobby and probably Priscilla and we stayed in a little house and went to the beach. Every two weeks I'd come to Miami and see him, and I had undivided attention and went to do something. It was always fun.

I think the billboard started around the time I was born, around '72. It's always been around my whole life. I don't remember my first memory of it.

I'd be with friends, or my cousin, Jim's daughter, and she always made a point to tell friends "that's her dad." I got over being embarrassed. I started working (at Don Bailey Carpet) in high school at 14 and until my son was born, I was bookkeeping and in the office. I did collections for the real estate. I haven't worked since seven years ago,

Last year we went to New York City with my son Adrian, who loves his grandpa, and my husband Roman, brother Bobby and his wife, and Donna and Don. We saw the Lion King. Don paid everything.

He's the most generous man in the world as far as I'm concerned.

He and Dondi take my son to UM baseball games. He caught a foul ball, and that was very exciting for him. He's taken him to the zoo and Lion Country Safari.

He spends money on other people and the only time he spends on himself is for vacations. I love the way he dresses and doesn't care. He's a great example. He's showing people don't worry about you house or car. He taught me by example that's all b.s.

One of the craziest memories from when I was a child: There was a baby shower or wedding shower, I came with mom, and we all went in and dad dresses up in all black and has a veil and walks in behind my mom at this party of women.

"Who in world is that?"

"I have no idea who she is."

We had been there awhile, and they kept looking at him and figured it out. "Oh, my God is that Don Bailey?"

I knew and I didn't say anything. It took at least 10 minutes.

He did same thing in Colorado at a friend's house, Hank Fineberg. Dressed as a woman and walked into the store and they didn't recognize my dad.

As for his Christmas cards, all I have to say about that is: Oh, my God.

BRETT BAILEY

Being the son of Don Bailey I'm sure is unlike any other growing experience or parental experience. He's just been a character my whole life.

And I didn't think it was weird. Or I don't even find it funny any more until now when I've lived away from them awhile because I went to college and I'm in law school.

I realized I had a very un-normal dad. When I was younger, I'd say to my friends, "Your dad doesn't get naked and run around? You dad doesn't scream obscenities?"

Whenever people would be around my parents, or my dad especially, they would laugh their a—off and I just never thought it was as funny as everyone else. I just thought that was normal. But now I'm starting to appreciate it a little bit more.

Another thing I like about being the son of Don Bailey is it gives you some sort of credibility. I'm realizing as I'm growing up if you meet somebody, I'm not just anybody. They'll go, "Oh, you're dad's that person on the sign?" And they'll immediately open up to you a little more because they associate you with somebody they like or grew up with. So that's always a good thing, too.

Growing up I guess I had trouble sleeping and I would ask someone to tell me a story. And instead of my mom doing it, after awhile my dad would say, "Donna, I've got this." And he'd come in. I must have been 6 years old, maybe even younger, when it started. But he would come in and start telling me bedtime stories.

What he would do, he'd take popular stories that were classics and catered to children, and he would put his twists to 'em. Like one story would be the story of the Dickless Horseman, and it'd basically be the headless horseman but he suffered the loss of his penis and it was just the adventures of the Dickless Horseman and his travels throughout this old land that my father created.

When my dad would take me to school he would always put on a tape of this comedian Tubby Boots, and he was a very vulgar comedian and I was in elementary school. And we'd be driving to school and he'd be telling jokes about hookers and being naked, very sexual, vulgar stuff.

I'd have my head full of this stuff walking into elementary school. I remember feeling like the coolest kid in the world because I'd be teaching all my friends curse words and what they mean and how to apply them, and all this grown up talk.

It made me be the naughty kid in school, though I never did it in front of teachers. Teachers didn't know. I guess I was trying to be the cool one among the kids because I knew all the dirty words. With those comedian tapes, I knew a lot of the jokes verbatim and my dad would alway ask me to tell them to his friends.

Another thing related to bedtime stories: One time, I think it was my dad's 60th birthday, he had a famous stripper there, a porn star. I don't know, some controversial erotic person. I think her name was Kathy Willits.

She was at his birthday party and he came home after his birthday party and I had a sleep over with my friend Daniel Cassis and he came in the bedroom and he was showing us pictures of him with this porn star. We're 6 or 7, he's showing us porno in our makeshift tent full of power rangers. I think it freaked Daniel out.

There was always something on our trips. We used to drive to Vermont after the whole 9-11 thing happened and we stopped flying as much. We had like a big conversion van, bucket seats, television. And we'd drive up to Vermont and stop at different areas along the way.

And just spending that much time with anybody you're going to see them, you're gonna see them do crazy things, especially my dad. We would be in the bathroom at a random truck stop, my dad would take out his pen and in the bathroom stalls write, "For a good time" and say a bunch of vulgar things and give my mom's cell phone number out underneath all that.

We would walk out laughing our assess off, and then mom would say, "What'd you guys do?"

What? Nothing.

And she'd just be getting these phone calls while she was driving up to Vermont. And me and my dad would laugh.

One road trip we were going to Orlando and I was with my friend Steve, and I rolled up a piece of paper and just stuck it in his ear real fast. And he hit the breaks and moved his whole body to the left, smacked his face as hard as he could and started yelling to my mom, "There's a bee! Get the freaking bee out of the car! Dammit."

Me and my friend were laughing so hard in the back seat and for 15 minutes he kept on, "We're going to die! There's bees everywhere!"

After we were laughing for longer we should have, he suspected it was probably me.

One time when I was around 8—this is three stories in one—he was going to get a new car and they were selling flavored ices at the dealership. He's negotiating with the guy for the truck, I'm like sitting there slurping this thing the whole time and he was getting bothered by it.

He said, "Brett, stop slurping that thing," Like getting all mad and that anger transferred over to the test drive. He's kind of already angry at me, I'm like slurping away and I just start laughing while we're in the test drive.

He said "Brett, why are you laughing? You were slurping, now you're laughing. You're disrespectful."

And I keep telling him, "Dad, you don't want to know why I'm laughing. Let it go. Just let it go." It was Dad, me in the middle and the guy that's selling us the car. And I just kept on laughing. And he's like "Brett, I'm pulling this car over. We've got to stop. This is very rude for the salesmen."

I told him, "Dad, just let it go. I can't stop laughing. You don't want this to be known."

And finally after the third time he was getting mad at me, I said "Dad, you balls are hanging out of your shorts, and they're as blue as the ocean. I'm sure the guy's been looking at it this whole time."

And I'm in the middle of these two guys. If you saw this image of this, it was unbelievable. It was amazing that he wasn't aware that his whole junk was outside of his shorts. And I'd be laughing and the guy would be talking about selling points about the truck and he would look over and glance at Dad's balls and a look of disgust would come over his face.

I guess Dad got embarrassed and angry about that—and it transferred over to this situation: Saying goodbye, talking to the dealer, he gets in his car and puts it in reverse and hits the gas and backs up into a brand new car on display.

Gets out of the car and starts yelling at the salesman, that it was his fault, which always happens. It's never his fault, it's always someone else's fault.

He screamed, "You motherf—! You put it in my f—blind spot! You crazy . . . What the hell? . . . I'm not going to pay for it! It's all your fault!"

Everybody was like so worried about how crazy he was being, they weren't even worried about the car. "Sir, don't worry about it. It's fine."

They were probably looking at him like this crazy man with his balls hanging out, you know thinking—we don't want to cause any problems, we just want him off this property.

It was a really interesting day.

Did he buy a new truck? I don't know.

Definitely not that day.

What must have happened is when he did buy it I wasn't around. I definitely wasn't included on the next trip.

The billboard is something I always knew. But like my first memories of it were when I was in middle school. I guess it didn't bother me because I always saw it as like what my dad did, and I didn't think twice about it.

It wasn't until my situation changed in middle school. Middle school's a very rough time for any kid, there's a lot of teasing and insecurities. So I was made aware of how people might not like it and poke fun, bring it up negatively.

And I remember my dad had these huge signs on the back of his pickup truck. It was like the length of his bed and four feet high. Both sides had his sign, huge advertisements of him lying naked to advertise his carpet business. Every time he'd take me to school, I'd make him pull over a couple of streets down from my school and go behind the building and have him drop me off there.

I would walk the rest of the way to school because I told him at the time, "Dad you can't drop me off with these signs with you naked on the side of the truck. People are going to think you're gay and they're going to make fun of me."

But now I realize that I was ridiculous, I really learned to love the signs. But I was very embarrassed for awhile.

We used to sneak in the movie theaters regularly. I think every Sunday my mom, my dad, my Uncle Jim, my Aunt Mary Ellen and I would go to the moves. The ritual would be we'd go to Lorenzo's Cafeteria and have a very nice and inexpensive meal and then go to the movies. And my dad would buy three seniors and one child, and my mom wouldn't be included or she'd be in one of the seniors.

There'd be one ticket that wasn't there. There'd be five of us and he'd get four tickets and say I was a child even though it happened until I was 16.

What happened was, he'd say, "Wait for a crowd, wait for a crowd," when we're waiting in line to go into the movie theater. As soon as there was a crowd he'd get all of us and like push us through and have us all say, "Oh, he has the ticket, he has the ticket."

And then we would all disperse. By the time he was done dealiing with the tickets, the ticket taker had no idea if there was four or five. It was a game for dad.

Then we'd get one large popcorn which had free refills, and a large soda which had refills, and courtesy cups and bring our own bags. So the ritual at the concession stand would be as soon as we bought our stuff we'd go over to the garbage can and pour out the popcorn into all the bags we brought, and pour the drinks in the different cups that were free, and then go back in line and refill it cause it was free.

He was always trying to save money, 'cause he would always bring up how he used to work for 10 cents an hour. That was the theme growing up. Always trying to get around ways of paying or save whenever you can.

There was one time we were going to the auto show and my dad saw how much parking was. He was like "These m—f—they think they can charge this much? We'll figure it out."

He hops this curb right in front of the Miami Beach Convention Center and then goes and parks instead of going through the guy to get the ticket. So we saved money there.

And then he saw how much it was to go in the car show.

"It's dah, dah, dah, just to go in to see a bunch of cars? Brett, follow me."

And we'd get to the exit of the Convention Center and he told me, "Brett, just walk backwards."

So we walked backwards through the exit of this place, and we go through and then someone grabs me and says "Hey, what are you doing?" I said "I don't know, man." I look and my dad is halfway gone. I'm like "Dad! Dad!"

And he screamed, "Brett, tell 'em I'm about to s— in m pants." And then I yank my arm from the guy and said, "I'm sorry, he has to go to the bathroom." And I ran.

And then we went in and we didn't have any other problems.

Stuff like that always happened.

I think it's amazing and it's unbelievable how much drive and how much persistence he has and he's still working. I've been on vacations with him and he doesn't feel right because he's not working. He's thinking about work, and I'm like envying his mindset 'cause when I'm on vacation and I'm enjoying it and I try to stay on vacation even when I'm in Miami.

He is all work all the time, which is a lot of the reason why he made it the way he did. He could have retired whenever he wanted but he wouldn't be happy. He doesn't want to do that. He likes to be efficient, he likes to be on top of things. He doesn't like other people handling things for him that he can handle himself.

I think growing up with no money made him never want to live through that again or have his children live through that. He sees spending money as forever gone out of his hands. So unless he absolutely needs it he's not going to spend for it. He used to always say, "Once you spend it, it's gone. You can't get it back or it's very hard to get it back under most circumstances." That's what he's always preached to me.

My dad and brother's push for excellence has affected me very positively. I am finishing my last semester at St. Thomas University (law school). I went undergrad to University of Miami. And I'm a disk jockey. I've deejayed in New York, South Beach, Baltimore, Memphis. I also do music production.

I've had a music studio almost nine years, and I have worked with a lot of artists and done a lot of song writing. I've worked with Pitbull and I've done some stuff with DJ Khaled and the Diaz Brothers. I hope to move forward on that.

At UM I majored in business management and my minor was in music business industry.

Due to my father's hard work, I was able to go to China and see the Olympics with my buddy Jeff and we were chilling with Evander Holyfield, 'cause my friend's dad was doing some business with Evander. Through him we met Chris Tucker, the move star from Money Talks and Rush Hour. He was there with Quincy Jones (my idol) whom I also met.

It obviously was a possibility for me to go in the family business. I mean, a father usually wants their son to follow up what they started. But ever since I was young I just had an interest in music.

I actually worked for the company at 83rd Street. I put in some hard work in the warehouse. I respect the people who work hard for our company. I'm only 24 and I knew like almost 10 years ago I wanted to be a producer, that is all I wanted to do. I've always had a background in music. I dance, I've played instruments. I've played at Carnegie Hall. It's always been my passion.

Being in the family business was kind of brought up earlier in my life but l was very stern that I wanted to do music when I was 12 of 13.

My dad said, "If you want to join the company, fine, whatever makes you happy, because you need to have piece of mind and do what you want to do. Don't let anybody force you."

One of the benefits of having him as a father—he always is trying to teach me something. Always. And growing up it was a bit annoying.

There has always been a lecture. Even now when he does, it still bothers me but I found that the years and years of repeating himself, and basically beating this information in my head has made me a much sharper person. I realize he's probably experienced more than a lot of people have because he grew up in an unfortunate situation and he has learned how to lose before he learned how to win.

He's had a lot of things happen to him for him to realize that's not the route to go, here's the right route. All these pitfalls he's constantly reminding me of and repeating ad nauseum have really made me a stronger person and have become my common sense.

I started realizing in undergrad and especially in law school how much an advantage I have compared to other people because I've had this information beaten in my head. People are losing money and doing stupid investments, doing this, doing that and think, "Why would you do such a thing? Don't you know what the situation might be?"

And I realize they don't know, they didn't have a father feeding all this information into their heads. So even now when he's lecturing I don't get annoyed. I know the benefit of it and I appreciate the nowledge he is passing on.

But it's definitely made me a much better person. Every day I think about it. There's always something happening each day where somebody has been and I think, Why would you do that? Then I realize that I only know the wise thing to do and am aware of what can happen because of him teaching me. I think he's one of the greatest dads for doing that, and for supporting my dreams and making me laugh.

DONNA BAILEY

Don and I met in 1976. I was 23 and he was 42. I don't remember the age difference being a big deal for me. I'd been married before and wasn't really looking for a serious relationship. And he was kind of on the fence on whether he was going to be permanently divorced.

The divorce was final, but he loved his family so much. Even though we dated a lot, he was still trying to patch up that marriage. Any special weekend he would still go home and be with his ex-wife and children. They still did family things together. Then after a few years of holidays apart we had enough; then we all did things together. He has been my best friend and most fun companion I could ever hope for.

We rarely spend time away from each other; it just doesn't feel right. I think we are a perfect fit—the kind of love you hope your children will find. We both give and take.

Back then Don wanted to spend holidays with everyone together. He didn't want the kids to choose who they would spend Christmas and Easter with, so we joined forces and everyone got together.

Christmases were with his ex-wife Johannah and her mother, the kids, and her boyfriend, and his mother. And they would all come over to our house Christmas morning. That was great. It was like a meshed family, never any problems.

I loved Johannah's mother Marvelyn. I'd go visit her with my son when he was little. I went skiing with his first wife, Gloria, and she and I got along great I got along great with both ex-wives because they were nice women and neither of them wanted him back, so there was no reason for me not to be friends with them. Possibly the reason they were not interested in renewing the relationship with Don is because he is tough, he can be very tough. But mostly, he is good. He's wonderful with his kids, he's wonderful to me, he's wonderful to his ex-wives. He's good to his employees. He's a good guy. He's complex, but he's a good guy.

I think of myself as the Gracie Allen and he's George Burns. You know, I'm the straight man. I'm the one that he bounces jokes off of.

He'll do a routine when we go on cruises. You know how you sit down at the table? He'll do a whole routine and I'd be the straight person, and it's usually really, really funny. So it's worth it and it makes for an interesting evening for us and our new friends.

All the kids are wonderful. We've had ups and downs with all of them. But they all respect their dad and he has them under control. He's still in control.

Now Don Junior, ha, you're not going to control Don Junior. But he respects him.

What is it like being married to Don Bailey? It's always fun. He's a lot of fun. People ask me, "Does he wake up being funny?" Yes. He goes to bed being funny. He's always pretty light-hearted when he's down, and he doesn't stay down for very long.

Recently he was sad about the passing of Jim Mandich (former Miami Dolphin and sportscaster). He took that hard. I mean, any time a close friend—when you're 78 and someone you know pretty well passes away—you take it personally. And so I felt for him. I could tell that he was off. He'll be off a few days over something like that. He's very sensitive.

Day to day he works. He works. We go on vacation, and we had a place in Vail and we decided we were going to stay for three or four weeks. It's beautiful in Vail in the summer. We thought this is perfect.

You hear of people taking off for the whole summer. We were there for about a week and a half and Don started following around the maintenance man of the resort to make sure he was doing his work. In the second week he starts finding out what real estate is for sale, whether it's a good buy. He pretends like he's going to buy this property, researches it. He can't stay inactive. It makes him nuts.

If we're on a cruise ship, he'll go to art auctions and research the different artists. He'll learn as much as he can. He can't sit still. He can't be dormant. He doesn't gamble—it would ruin his trip if he lost money. He doesn't drink much unless it comes with it. When we get off the ship he'll try to sell carpet.

We got off in Belize, a country that has no money. Nobody has money there. He went to the different places and tried to sell them remnants. So he was selling carpet in Belize with open sewers instead of relaxing at the beach.

The billboard: The first day I met him was at a wedding. He and Don Junior went to the wedding of the next door neighbor, Kim, who was a friend of mine from college. I was in town because I was going through a divorce and staying with another girl friend. Everyone was going to the wedding. Kim dropped by the night before and said, "Donna, come to the wedding tomorrow." I said, "OK but I don't have anything to wear." So I borrowed a dress. I showed up at this wedding with six other girlfriends and as we drove up so did Don. He had a fancy car, an Excaliber, with a smaller version of his billboard sign on the back of it. The girls in the car turned to me and said, "Don't have anything to do with that guy. He is awful. He's a notorious womanizer. Bad news."

I said, "OK, that's kind of weird, that sign. Whatever." I went to the wedding and the reception and I'm enjoying myself when Don approached me. I came from West Palm Beach and the people I hung around with were hippies or rednecks. So guys mostly wore jeans and T-shirts or a suit.

Don had a leisure suit on. He had matching pants and shirt that wasn't tucked in and clogs. I didn't even know what to think of what he had on. It was just too bizarre. It was 1976, the disco era.

So here was this guy in this weird outfit, but he seemed charming. He said, "We're all going somewhere for a drink afterward. Would you like to go?" This is what we now describe as our "Some Enchanted Evening" moment.

I had met Don Junior at the bar; he was 14. I had brothers that age. So I saw this imp of a kid over there trying to sneak a drink and I talked to him and was kidding around with him. When I saw that those two are connected, I immediately thought Don must have something special going on because his kid was awfully cute.

We were getting ready to leave the reception and Don said, "I've had too much to drink, would you like to drive my car?" And I said, "OK, I'll drive." When the car came around and I saw that it was the car with the sign on the back, I said, "Oh, my God, my girlfriends told me to stay away from you. I can't believe this happened. They're going to think I deliberately tried to meet you. I doubt they will even talk to me now."

He said, "Why? I'm a nice guy."

And he was a nice guy, and the rest is history.

I had no clue what that billboard meant. Although I did know Burt Reynolds. His niece went to school with me in Riviera Beach, so we had slumber parties at Burt's house when we were growing up. Never saw him. He was in California at the time, but he had a house in Lake Park. We would hang out there and go to the screening room and look at all his old movies.

Burt's niece, Nancy, came to a reunion and I said, "You know I'm dating Don Bailey who uses Burt's pose on his signboard."

She said she mentioned it to Burt because she was working with her mother for Burt. He thinks it's very funny, which explains why there has never been anything negative coming from his camp about Don's signboard.

Don and Burt have mutual friends, like Lee Corso. I don't think Burt thinks it's a big deal. I have heard he is a very nice man. And he's probably heard that Don's a nice man.

One problem I have with Don is when he is like a little 12-year-old in church who misbehaves. When he's in a situation where he is supposed to act a certain way, he loves being naughty. So those are the only times I've had—you know, church functions, fancy parties, fundraisers anywhere he's supposed to act appropriately is usually when he will act up. Sometimes it is horrible. He will be the most bizarre he can be. He likes to say, "Do you want someone boring or someone who will entertain you?" Honestly I will take the entertainment even if it means being embarrassed some of the time.

He is a free spirit and has the quickest wit I have ever been around.

We recently met Bill Clinton at a fundraiser. We were about to have our picture taken when Don said, "Hey, Bill, sorry I couldn't make Chelsea's wedding—we were busy." Clinton did a double take and posed for the picture laughing.

Don requires everyone around him to be responsible. If you are asked to do something, as in the list I get—or notes, they need to be done. End of story. To me it seems like the least I could do for the wonderful life he has provided me with. I get to play tennis, do fundraising for my church, our son's schools, Ronald McDonald House and work in my travel business. And in return he asks me to do a few things. Usually related to Real Estate since I have been his personal R.E. Broker since 1978. Well worth it. I love my life.

Don and Don Junior are incredibly close, and the fact that he has trusted Don Junior's judgment in the running of the carpet business—that's rare in a father-son business relationship. He really has faith in him and appreciates the work ethic and responsibility Don Junior has taken on.

They're also good friends. They enjoy each other's company. They spend time together because they want to. Not because they have to. They've had disagreements, but very few. I think that's because they are both respectful and understanding of each other.

The relationship with Bobby has always been very good. It took him awhile to find his niche in this family business and he's found it. He is the brightest bulb. He is a great natural athlete and was so fun to watch in high school sports. We enjoyed great trips with Bob to Africa and Japan, where even though he was in his teens he had to figure the currency and language for us.

Jeanne was a bit of a challenge growing up. But Don has enjoyed having a daughter. We had some great vacations with her in New York City. She is red-headed and we would walk into the lobby at the Plaza hotel and the piano player would play the song from Annie. We always tried to plan something special when we had her for the weekend and Don would play tag or whatever game she wanted to play for hours. He was putty in her hands. It was very sweet.

He loves all his children. They are all unique and they always get along with very little drama.

And the youngest one, Brett, we overindulge and we over-talk about him. You get Don started and he'll never stop. And he does this in front of the other kids.

What I think is remarkable is that the three other kids have been so kind to the youngest, even though we have shoved him down their throats. We just can not say enough about our baby boy. It's embarrassing how much we adore that kid. And he's not without faults. He's pretty special right now, he's shining bright both artistically and scholastically.

Don's joy now is the grandson, Adrian. Jeannie has an 8-year-old. Don will find out what he likes to do and take off from a busy day. When most men Don's age might go home and take a nap, he'll take Adrian to Chucky Cheese and play games. I have to watch Don at Chucky Cheese because he likes to ask for leftover pizza from parties like he is some kind of homeless person who cannot afford to pay for a meal. He gets a big kick out of this. He even asks for the leftover cake. Just like he did with Brett, he will talk to Adrian and use naughty words and act rude. Sometimes it is hard to identify the child. He will do anything to entertain him and make him feel special. And the little boy lights up when he sees him, and that's all Don wants, that bright smile,

There's a photo displayed in our condo of Don with all three wives. Unusual, I guess. Unusual because that picture was taken at our wedding reception. It was a pool party, it was the day after our wedding. Even though I'd been with him eight years, I just really wasn't comfortable with his three kids going to a big wedding with their dad. We had a small ceremony with family at the Fontainebleau on Miami Beach and the next day was the 4th of July. This meant a wonderful annual pool party at the Galpins in Miami Shores. All our friends were there so we called it our wedding reception. Johannah, the second wife, and Gloria, the first wife, were there and the picture was taken by the pool in our bathing suits. Don loves that picture.

We three women attended many events together over the years. There was one night that our host made up T-shirts for all the women to wear. Most women got T-shirts that read, NO, I'VE NEVER BEEN MARRIED TO DON BAILEY.

The two ex-wives had T-shirts that read, YES, I'VE BEEN MARRIED TO DON BAILEY.

And mine said, HIS MONEY. WHY ELSE? It was pretty funny . . .

Usually Don is the comic. He's a very good ad libber. People enjoy him.

I went to a carpet convention and I'm walking down the hallway with him and all the guys are coming out of their booths and falling down laughing. The minute they look at him they start laughing.

And I'm looking to see if he has a funny hat on, or is he making faces? Why are these people laughing? I said, "What is the deal?"

And he said, "I've done some crazy stuff at these carpet conventions and they all remember me."

At the business, he always looks at the guys at the bottom, more than the salesmen that are making the big money. He's been the hero of the warehousemen. And what I see, it gives him no better joy. He seeks it. He gives them money, he buys them things.

The guy who does our yard, he bought him a car. Christmas morning Don had to check on something at the store and he saw our yard man walking alone on Biscayne Blvd. The guy's name is Precious.

Don said, "Precious, what are you doing on this Christmas morning?"

Precious said, "I'm going to have some breakfast."

Don said, "Let me buy you breakfast."

When he takes him to breakfast Don finds out his car's not working, that his wife left him, he's served time and he might be going back. This is really a sweet man, he's just had some bad luck. Don decides he should buy him a truck, to get him a better running truck.

So Don was late for brunch with the whole family because he was out looking for a new truck for Precious the yardman. Typical story. He loves to help the underdog . . .

The first night I met him, there was some kid selling candy bars outside the bar we were going into, and Don said, "How many candy bars have you got?" The kid says, "I've got 10." Don says, "What are you going to do with the money?" He says, "I'm going to buy my mom a present. Tomorrow is Mother's Day."

And Don said, "OK, I'm going to buy all these candy bars but you keep the candy and you better get your mom a present." And the kid goes, "OK."

And right then I thought, wow, this is somebody different. This is a different kind of a guy. It's amazing. And he says no one ever helped him out, no one ever gave him a break when he was starting out. He's pretty special.

Johannah's Comments

(As told to Don Junior)

She said, "The best thing Don did for me was give me my three children." She feels that's the greatest gift he gave her. She kept coming back to that. She said the marriage was great because the kids were great. And the struggles were what young people go through.

And she talked about how hard he worked and how he provided for the family and how he made sure after the divorce—before, during and after—that the kids had the right education. Both my brother and sister went to private schools. He was an excellent provider

Son Brett with Donna and Don.

Don Junior and Don.

Daughter Jeannie and Don.

Don and grandson Adrian with his first trophy.

8. FRIENDS

DICK BARTLETT

Don and I go back. We were together at Expressway Carpet before he formed Don Bailey Carpet in 1971. I joined him in 1969. I was with Eastern Airlines. He had two partners, Jim Flack and Mike Solon at Expressway, and I knew Flack.

It's been a lot of laughs, been wonderful. He just keeps me laughing all the time. He's like my brother. I see him more than my brother. I retired in 2005 and live In Ormond Beach.

Don is like the Energizer battery. He never quits. He's too much.

The first time we actually met was at his partner Flack's wedding in Michigan. It was the first date I had with my wife. She lived there and I lived in Bermuda.

I met Don at the airport and drove to pick her up and drove to the small town where Jimmy Hoffa lived.

Don was in the wedding party. Of course we partied pretty hard. The preacher told them at rehearsal if they're in the same condition tomorrow he wouldn't marry them.

We went back to the hotel and had more drinks. Don thought he was Superman in underwear with a shower curtain around his shoulders running up the streets in front of hotel. That was my wife's first impression of him. Her being a school marm, she was taken aback.

We opened Don Bailey Carpets in '71, with small store off 7th Avenue, just he and I. It was not more than 5,000 square feet, maybe smaller.

A few things that happened there: George Allen was hired as a salesman, and he had drinking problem and would sneak out to his car and have a nip. One time while he was waiting on a lady with a baby in a stroller, Don said his breath was so bad it put the baby to sleep. The baby was quiet as a mouse.

When the carpet trucks came in to unload, he and I unloaded by hand and put them on dollies and in warehouse. And we unloaded an entire tracker trailer of padding. It was quite a mess.

The way we got started, most of the inventory came from Carpets Systems. We knew the owner, Jasper Williams, and he'd give us leftover pieces and there was no cash investment. It was on consignment. We'd pay him when we sold.

The highlight of that store was when we sold the Republican and Democratic conventions in Miami Beach. We sold the red carpet three times. The third was to the public. We put it in a dumpster outside and a customer said could he buy it, and he knew it was used, for a room or garage. So we started selling it.

Then we moved up to the store Junior is in now on 148th street, around 1974. It was 10 times bigger than the one we had. And we had our own inventory there.

One night while we were closed some guy had a heart attack and his car came right through the wall and ended up in our showroom. Don said, "Call the insurance company quick. Let's see what we can get."

One time we had a kid driving the fork lift with a lift in front, and somebody was in the bathroom and the pole went through the wall over a guy's head. It startled him, kind of.

Don always was on the alert for additional income. After renting some of the offices he added a second floor over our showroom to rent more space. Somebody told him, "You're wasting space," so we put a huge office upstairs and rented it out to a church.

Regarding the billboard, I told everybody that's his head and my body. I thought it was great. Anything to draw the attention we needed.

In an ad you can do a child or pretty girl, and I said, "But a pretty guy?"

He loves to make money, never has enough. It's a challenge with him, it's the thrill. He gets real satisfaction in turning the dollars.

He was really good to me. I didn't have that intuition to making dollars like he did. My forte was selling.

We go on trips all the time together. We went with Johannah to Kitsbul, Austria, on a ski trip. The tour we were on we flew in on one of the cheap airlines, of course. A bus picked us up for a six-hour ride. The bus opened the door after six hours and left us there and we had no idea where we were.

We had to carry our bags an hour to an hour and a half and it's freezing cold to get to a pension. It was very nice once we got there.

We were walking down the road by pension with another couple and Don was gonna hit a guy in the head with a snow ball, and it was ice, not snow. It was a snowball that was ice.

We went sleigh riding, took these sleds and walked up to the top of a mountain. They said it's a short walk. We walked for two hours pulling a sled.

On the way up there was a guy there and we asked him if we're going in the right direction.

Don said, "Me. Us." He's moving his hands. "We want to go up mountain. Are we going . . . ?" and he points up the mountain.

And the guy said, "What's wrong with you? Don't you speak English?"

After sledding and skiing we were taking them to town to turn them in, and the sled went off edge of bridge and it had a rope and I'm trying to pull it up and bending over and my jeans are slipping off. And Don's drawing a crowd and pointing and 10 people watching me. I was embarrassed but it wasn't the first time.

We went to Interlochen, Switzerland, and there were about 100 carpet dealers from all over the U.S. We had a formal evening at a beautiful hotel ballroom that was 700 years old. We went to our table and sat down and Don was missing.

They brought the first course and we're drinking wine and having a good time. I look back and here comes a nun into the room, and it's

Don with the nun's outfit and he's carrying a cross around his neck. He's got nun shoes, everything. All you could see was his face.

It cracked the whole place up. He said, "It wasn't so bad wearing the outfit except I got attacked by two priests in the elevator."

The next day we took a train trip to the top of a mountain to the Ice Palace. It's a whole city carved out of ice. And we're missing Don again. I turn around and there he is on edge of the ice with pants down mooning everybody.

Never a dull moment.

We went to Jamaica on a cruise, went to Dunn's River Falls, a big tourist attraction. We climbed up the falls, everything is beautiful, and coming down they have these little booths with women braiding their hair.

We went back to the ship and met at the pool, and Don comes out and he's got a Rastafarian wig hanging out of his bathing suit and says, "I got my hair braided, too."

Another night on the ship we're all in the casino and everybody is dressed up, and he comes in with a cape and Jockey shorts and sunglasses and the Rastafarian wig. The female manager threw him out.

Another time we're on the Orient Express from London. We get on and we have a suite with a table in between and chairs around it. They serve champagne and orange juice in the morning before they serve breakfast on the beautiful table with china and crystal.

There was a silver vase with flowers in it, and Donna says to Don, "See if you can buy the vase, it's $200." Don says, "It's too much."

We went to a castle, the Cliffs of Dover, and when we got back Don had a trench coat on. After we got out of the station he says, "Remember that vase?" The trench coach has it and the flowers are still in it.

I said, "They'll remember our table."

And he said, "Remember that bitchy couple? I took it off their table."

During Hurricane Andrew (in 1992) he came to my house in Miami Lakes, shows up with that vase 10 years later and gives it to my wife. And a bottle of Dom Perignon.

We had a hurricane party at my house. It was great. We never lost power because we had underground lines.

A funny story: When his mom got sick, I think Alzheimer's, Don wanted to borrow her car. She gave him they keys and after that she called the police and said her car had been stolen. She'd forgotten she gave him the keys.

When she got sick in bed, Don would visit her all the time, and she would say, "Thank you, Jimmy," and never acknowledge him. After many visits he convinced her it's him and she bit his hand.

He came to my daughter's wedding and he stayed at my house a couple weeks. We went to the wedding with Don and my mother. She looked at Don and said, "Who is that man?" She had the same thing his mother had.

It's been fun ride. I've enjoyed all these years.

HANK FINEBERG

We had some really unbelievable experiences. I was just talking to a mutual friend and I laughed so hard I cried on the phone.

I don't know how much you can print.

The first day Don and I met, I was married to Harry Rich's daughter. We moved to Florida in 1959 and I started to work at Harry Rich.

Don's five years older than me. Both of us before we met were the craziest, horniest guys. The first day we met at Rich we went across the boulevard and had lunch and immediately hit it off. Don says, "You want to get laid? And we go to some hooker he knew. From then on it was total insanity. So many times we had these crazy laughs.

At Expressway Carpet, he'd get naked all the time. Each room was like a showroom, and I'm in this little room and a customer is on the other side. Don suddenly appears in the doorway naked and says, "Did you show her this?" The woman can't see him and as she turns around he disappears.

Another time in the doorway he farts, like an explosion. The lady doesn't know whether he did it or I did it and he disappeared.

He'd always drop his pants in a restaurant. We'd go to Atlanta for a show for carpet buyers and reps. A market. It was just a free for all and a crazy party time. We just went nuts.

We're in this nice restaurant one night and standing in the salad bar line and people are dressed nice. Don drops his pants to his ankles . . . and I'm thinking we're gonna get taken to jail.

As we're leaving the restaurant, at the lower level, there was a hostess there and we're walking up the stairs and not paying attention to Don and he said something and he's halfway up stairs and his pants are down to his ankles

Everywhere we go I'm thinking we're not gonna get out of here without getting arrested.

We were best friends. I was outside the hospital room when Don Junior was born. He's like a second son. We have an incredibly close relationship.

My wife and I have been together 30 years and she says, "You and Don are like Siamese twins. The stuff you guys did is not printable."

Don and his ex-wife, when they finally divorced, one scene pushed it over the top. I think Don was out late at night and he was drunk and had a girl in a motel on Biscayne Boulevard and for some reason he had to run across street with no pants on. His mother-in-law was driving up the street and he ran right in front of her car. He tried to deny it.

We're in Atlanta one time and they had just completed the Hyatt Regency, where they have glass elevators. It's really nice. Don loved to drop his pants in a glass elevator and people would freak out. By the time anybody could get to him he'd disappear.

One time I'm walking to my room and I look down one to two levels and I see a girl laughing hysterically and Don is chasing her naked.

It was just endless.

When Dondi was playing with the Hurricanes, I was living out here in Colorado. The really wild and crazy times were before that.

When I was working at Packer Pontiac one day one of these guys had a girl who wanted to party and I called Don. I think he at was at Rich and he races down. I had to go outside and Packer Pontiac had an open showroom and the offices were totally open to the showroom. Another nut job: I walk around the corner, Maury Gross has his pants down and the girl has got her blouse up and Don is with his pants down.

I couldn't believe what I was seeing. If the owner comes down and sees this we'll all be arrested and fired.

He's the funniest guy. He could've made millions as a comedian. Unbelievable.

I had a little clothing store, a tall and big man store, and I hear the door open and I see this scary looking cross-dressing nurse in a white nurse uniform, wig, the whole nine yards. As soon as I recognized it was Don, I was hysterical.

He showed up as a nun a lot.

One of my younger sons graduated from high school and my mother was there. It was the middle to the late 1980s, and Don shows up in wig and complete silk Elvis outfit. He's just totally insane.

Every Wednesday night the carpet people from Miami would meet at a bar and restaurant. They had a buffet and it was real crowded. Guys and girls there. And a friend was telling me that one day Don said, "Look down." And his pants were down, but nobody could see because it was so crowded.

Don first of all is one of the smartest guys, and I've never known anybody who works as hard as Don to this day. He works six days a week and goes to the Keys and goes to work on Sunday.

When I first came to Harry Rich, when he was 23 and Rich made him the manager of the store, that store was largest carpet store in the country. It was an unbelievable store.

I've never met a better business person and harder worker, and besides that he's always been a real generous and kind person. He's still helping people, taking people in that other people think are losers and they become manager of the store.

I love him. I have two best friends and he is one of them.

The billboard: He and wife and me and my wife were together and we see the spread of Burt Reynolds in Cosmopolitan. And I had a picture of me laying in this position and we're cracking up and he said, "You ought to do it." And I said, "You should do it."

He got his brother to paint the billboard. Jack put Don Bailey's face on it.

I sold carpet to a woman here in Boulder four or five months ago, and she said she's from Miami and this crazy guy had a billboard, and I take out his business card which has the photo of the billboard. She says, "My God, he was crazy."

I remember Don had a '56 T-bird, turquoise, with a Continental kit on the back. And he and I go out cruising and we'd always go down to Liberty City to the Mr. James Club, and the King of Hearts. We were the only white people there but Don knew a lot of the people. We had some great times.

One night we were going home real late and Don lost his pants and had no underwear. He never wore them. He says, "How am I gonna go in the house? How am I gonna explain to Johannah?

I said, "Pour beer all over you and she'll think you smashed. That's the only way you get away with it."

I don't remember what outcome was but he lived through it.

Harry Rich was an amazing human being. I'd moved down from the north and I never had seen segregated bathrooms. The Dade County building inspectors would come by, and if you did not have separate drinking fountains and bathrooms you would get tickets and citations. And Rich always refused, saying he was not going to degrade his friends and employees. A lot of his family was in Austrian concentration camps. He'd never participate in segregation. They'd give him hell and say, "You can't do that." And he'd say, "Go ahead and arrest me. I'll take it to the Supreme Court."

Don one time was standing there at Expressway Carpet, and one of the women who worked for him had little white poodle. We had all the carpet remnants standing up against the wall if we wanted to show them. The dog would pee on the remnants.

One day I'm showing an elderly couple and the dog comes up and pees on my leg and the remnants, and Don cracked up hysterically.

The really juicy stuff I've left out. We were crazy, I don't know how we got away with it. Everybody involved was having a great time., hysterical hold-your-sides laughter.

HERB DAVIS

We grew up in the same neighborhood and I've known him since he was 6 or 7 or 8. Don has always been comical like he is now. He hasn't changed.

Always cheap. I don't know if that's a joke or for real, to be frank. We both still drive trucks after all these years. He says, "I see you don't have automatic windows either. But we have moved up to automatic transmission."

When we were young, only like 17, we'd go to a nightclub down in Miami, the Gaiety Club on 78th and Biscayne. This girl dancer, Rita, would dance with a boa or python and strip and dance. There would be five or six of us there.

One time we were putting back $1 tips and I look back and Don is picking up one of the dollars and he said, "I don't have enough money."

Another time we went there and we didn't have enough money.

He said he was born really poor, but his mom and dad had a grocery store. In my day he wasn't considered poverty like he wants people to believe.

At the time we didn't realize we were poor, we had such a great time in our childhood. I'm thankful we're still friends,. I call him four or five times a year and see him occasionally.

I went to his store on 7th Avenue where Junior is at. They had a lot of redwood tables and one caught my eye. It was five inches thick and five to six-feet long. I asked Don how much it is and he said $1,000. I said, "What?"

I went out to California and fell in love with redwoods. I said, "I'll give you $500. He said, "Nah, can't sell it,"

I said, "There's no way you're going to let me leave here without it," and set $500 on table, and he took it.

On Saturday nights we'd go to my cousin's house, Raymond, at 56th Street and 7th Avenue. On 54th was Monty's all-night open restaurant. We were probably 16 years old at the time.

He once said, "I'm on the University of Miami football team. You know the guy with the bucket of water and towels? The waterboy? I can't even carry that. I'm the guy that washes the towels, I'm not good enough to carry the water."

He is funny with everyone.

Joe Brodsky and I and Don were close friends, I got away from the group when I graduated from ninth grade and felt I didn't need any more education. Don always was a smart kid and always did well in school, as far as I know.

We had the same teachers and classes. He was always a good friend and I am honored to be his friend.

After all these years I wake up and thank God we're still here. I love him and know he loves me. Some things I can't tell you. We had a great time.

I was raised not by a real father but by uncles. I never felt I missed anything in life. I was blessed to be in the same neighborhood as Don.

I thought the billboard was kind of silly at the time, but he's cashed in. His body never looked that good, don't b.s. me. It turned up even last year. I said, "Do you know you got Billboard of the Year in the Keys" in *Florida Keys* magazine? He didn't know it.

I saw a picture of Don Junior in a UM uniform and he looked exactly as Don looked but Don wasn't as tall or as lean. He was always a little on the paunchy side.

I contribute his longevity and health to his being a happy person. He's always good to his employees. I've heard that.

I couldn't be happier for anybody. It's been a great 70 years and I hope we have 70 more.

DAVID RICH

I'm the son of Harry Rich. Don is five years older than me and is a natural salesman, and he became number two in the company. He's a super salesman and an engaging personality.

And, of course, a little crazy.

Some stories I'd rather not have published. Don took me to Cuba at 16 in the mid-1950s. It was an unusual place to go. We went from Key West. A round trip ticket was $10 each. I learned a side of the world I learned about later through Hemingway.

Socially I've know him a minimal amount. I went to the University of Florida and graduated and never worked directly with Bailey. I worked with another company in the late '60s when he quit and opened his own business. I closed down the company when my father retired in 1998.

The billboard was an extremely clever marketing move and ahead of his time. Everybody asked me if he looks like that. It helps his visibility tremendously. He's always been a good marketer.

Don had a surprise 60th or 70th birthday party, and Ferdie Pacheco was the emcee. He's better than John Stewart of today.

My father taught him everything about marketing and sales. He's Horatio Alger for real.

He was a wild man around the ladies in his younger days. He was just crazy. I'm surprised he didn't get arrested.

One time Bailey and I and two other people went out for a drink and he went to the men's room and was gone for a very long time. I went to find him and found out he left out of a window so he wouldn't have to pay his bill. He's outside laughing like hell. I said, "Give me the $2," but he wouldn't.

I want an autographed copy of his book. And I'm not paying for it.

JOYCE BRODSKY

My husband Joe and Don were very good friends. They shared a lot of crazy experiences together.

Don is a dear, dear person but he never ceases to shock. I think that's how he gets his kicks, in laughing and making people laugh. And doing crazy things and shocking people. The Christmas card epitomizes Don Bailey.

He's the dearest, sweetest man and I love him and his wife Donna, and Dondi and Priscilla.

Don had known Joe since they went to high school and he wanted Don Junior under his tutelage when he was head coach at Hialeah-Miami Lakes High. Joe eventually went to the University of Miami with Lou Saban and Don played at the U.

They were close, Joe being in football and that being very demanding, they didn't spend a lot of time together. For awhile Joe was at the University of Florida and Don was here.

It's not like they got together a lot after high school. And Joe came back to Miami and football was 24 hours a day.

Then Joe and I were out of town for 10 years in Dallas (with the Cowboys), but we didn't lose contact with Don.

He never ceases to amaze me. He's a wonderful person at heart. Generous, kind. I don't know how many jobs he gave to a person in need for a job. He has a heart of gold,

The billboard symbolized Don Bailey. That's him through and through.

Some stories I remember I don't want printed. That's a story in itself.

Some people kind of meld into another's personality, but there's only one Don Bailey Senior.

If Joe were alive, he could write a book. Unfortunately I can't write that book.

Don's is an amazing story. I remember he cleaned toilets at Harry Rich, and years later he owned Harry Rich. He is an amazing person.

Joe was fiercely loyal to his friends, and Don is too.

SISTERS RITA GILCHRIST and AUDREY CRAWFORD

RITA

Both of us have known Don for eons. Audrey's husband worked with Don. I met him through my sister. We're from a family of five girls and one went to school with Don, and Audrey became friends with Don. She went through all his marriages with him and I tagged along because they are just a funny, funny crew. And I worked for Don. He just walks in the door and I start laughing. He's one of the funniest persons I've known. And I just adore Dondi. I grew up with Dondi, too. We're just all very close,

I went to work for Don in 1970 and he sent me to Dallas. He had a road show. I'd find a warehouse and he'd send remnants. We were in

Tyler and we had no electricity and Donald said, "Well, certainly you have a flashlight." I said, "There's no air conditioning and electricity there."

We marched in with flashlights, and people were fighting over the remnants. A man said, "I was here first" and ripped the sleeve off my arm. I started crying and I'm standing with a flashlight. Don came over and said, "You don't cry when you have customers, you cry when you don't have customers." It's so Donald. He won't miss a lick of business no matter what the sales people had to go through.

Another story that's very much a part of Donald: He said, "I'll take care of the guy (who ripped my sleeve)." Don leaned over and farted the loudest and hardest I've ever heard and winked at me. I said, "You think you got even but I'm the one that had to smell that."

He was just a character and a half, the most colorful person I think I'll ever meet in my life.

Donald loves Mexican food. There was a restaurant by my apartment complex, and all the kids had hot sauce and onions and carrots. It looked pretty good. You'd take the tortilla and fill it with the food. Unbeknown to me it was hot jalapeno pepper juice. I ate it and couldn't get any words out. I did the same thing to Donald and his mouth was on fire. Any time he brought people to town he'd want to take them that restaurant to fire them up.

One night we went out to dinner with 10 people. I fell asleep at the table and he left me with the check. I didn't think it was funny but he did. He said, "That'll teach you to fall asleep when we have business people to entertain."

I was totally not surprised about the billboard and very glad he put on a flesh colored bathing suit so that he had something on. And years later, after I'd lived around the world and moved back to Florida two years ago, I was taking a bus to Miami on a tour. The bus is going down this street and there's his billboard and everyone on bus starts laughing. I didn't tell them I knew him and that he's a lot older than that now.

Donald is the most giving person you'd ever want to meet. He doesn't horde his success, he rewards the people who work for him. He's kind.

His success story is that he's such a hard worker. He's played as hard as he worked, and he does both well. You're not allowed to not laugh when you're around Donald.

We had a friend who had an emergency colonoscopy. Donald went in to visit him with a skateboard and giant black heavy duty garbage bag with a ribbon around it and said, "This will make you feel better. Wheel this next to you, drop it in here. You don't have to miss anything." And he gave him a fly swatter. Who in the world would think of it or do it to a friend? He has that knack to get away with it.

But he's crying on the inside and you know he's feeling your pain. But we feel it in a different way because you laugh about it.

That's our Donald. He is unique. There will never be another Don Bailey.

AUDREY

I've known Don for 60 years. There were five girls in our family. My sister Patty must have been going to school with him at Jackson. We'd moved from Houston, Tex. My sister and I are in a pizza parlor and Don came in and my sister said, "Oh, there's Don Bailey." I was only about 14 or so. His dad owned a grocery store and right next door was a pharmacy with a soda fountain, and Don worked there and I got a job at the soda fountain. The Bailey brothers would come in and chat every once in awhile. I was working there about a year when I met my husband and he knew Don real well because they all lived in the neighborhood.

Don is just a character and a half. I was very good friends with his first wife, second and third. I was maid of honor at his first wedding in June, 1956.

We've just been good friends over the years. I've been married three times and he knew all three of my husbands. I never dated him or worked for him, we've just been friends.

When he was married to Johannah we used to go out all the time. And one morning she was cooking breakfast for the kids and a taxi drove up to the house. Don had a towel wrapped around him and he asked her to come out and pay the taxi driver. He'd gotten robbed from a black hooker. That was the straw that broke the camel's back for their marriage.

One time there was a restaurant in the southwest section called The Depot and he took a whole group of friends. After dinner he said he was going to the restroom and he would meet us out front. They had an old train luggage cart in front of restaurant, and when we got up to leave he was in the cart naked and leaning on his elbow like the billboard pose. It was hysterical.

I remember a funny trip. Johannah and Sammy, my first husband, and Don's friend, the four of us went to Mexico on vacation and we went to this health ranch, when I about 19 years old. Donald got the tourist trots really bad, and we were riding horses on wooden saddles and he was crying and screaming that he had to go to the bathroom. It was hysterical.

We went to a place with health food and health baths and he was so sick he asked Johannah to call his mother. You'd pay the hotel by the day. He asked if there was any chance he'd get a refund because he wasn't able to eat for three days.

We were really surprised he did the billboard. He was talking about it and he'd say most anything and you didn't know he'd do it. And all of sudden they were everywhere. Only Don would do that.

We had another couple we ran around with, Peggy and Dick Gonzalez, and she had a dinner party and one of her best friends had just married a man who had been a priest. Don never appeared without a grand entrance, and he bought a priest outfit and big cross to put around his neck and an evening purse on his arm. Peggy got a laugh but her best friend, who was married to the ex-priest, got up and said, "We're leaving," and they never spoke to each other again. The rest of us got a big laugh.

I've know his family, parents, brothers, and they're all wonderful people and they had no money at all and his dad always worked hard. But Don was truly a self-made millionaire, so to speak, although he did very well in the carpet business but made a lot in real estate and investments.

It's a wonder what he's done and he has always been a truly generous and friendly person. He's a good friend and I can't say enough about him. I've loved all three of his wives. They're all great, very nice women. Johannah and I became really close friends.

Don never wears socks or underwear. The reason he has so much money now is because he never spent it on socks and underwear.

DICK GONZALEZ

One time we had a dinner party at my house, and a number of couples were there. This was in the era when streaking was popular. You'd be watching a baseball game and some guy would be streaking naked, or at a football field, and it was a big thing. As the evening wore on, we'd all drank quite a bit and somebody mentioned to Don, "I dare you to streak around the block." He said, "I won't streak around the block but I'll go down to the corner and back."

So he goes right to the front door, takes off his clothes, leaves them at the door and goes running naked down the street. This is about midnight or 1 o'clock in the morning. He goes down to the corner, and when he's coming back—my house is on the other corner—he's approaching my house. My neighbor is walking his dog, and my neighbor was president of the Optimist Club and Don had his application pending for membership in the Optimist Club. And my neighbor sees him naked and they spoke to each other. And the next day my neighbor says, "That Bailey boy is quite a guy." I said, "It was a dare." He was understanding about it. My neighbor was Lucian Renuart, who owned a lumber company.

When my daughter was born, my wife's girlfriends gave her a baby shower. And it was all women at the shower and Don came dressed as a woman, with a dress, high heels, a wig. A lot of the girls knew him and it was hilarious but some of the women didn't know him. One of my neighbors who didn't know him asked my wife, "Who is that ugly woman?"

He didn't have any underwear on and he sat on the couch and he was somewhat exposed when he crossed his legs. A woman who didn't know who he is was stunned.

I had a friend who came from a very privileged, wealthy background—a mansion in Palm Beach, a home in the Hamptons—a lot of money. You'd think of him being a straight-laced guy but he really wasn't. We went out with him and his wife one night and Don and his wife Donna, and I had warned Don. It was the first time he was meeting him. I said, "Be careful because I don't know if he would take to some of your humor." Don said, "Don't worry, I'll be very proper." So we're having dinner and everybody's talking, three couples, and Don had just moved into the Cricket Club and he was telling us how beautiful the apartment was, with a beautiful balcony. He said, "As a matter of fact, the balcony is so beautiful when I come home from work on Saturday afternoon my wife and I usually engage in intercourse on the balcony. We stopped doing it when we noticed that every Saturday there would be a helicopter hovering over. They probably knew our schedule."

My friend and his wife loved him. They would invite him all the time because they got such a kick out of him. They were shocked at first and then they got used to him.

One night during the winter years ago, it was very cold and we had gotten all dressed up to go out to dinner. There was a very popular night club on Biscayne Boulevard down near the Omni called Les Violins. It was a copy of the night club in Havana, it was very popular with Latins and with Cubans and it was beautiful, with a good restaurant. We're dancing on the dance floor and I look over at Don and Donna and they had switched shoes. He had on her high heels and she put on his boots, and there they are dancing the maranga and people are looking at him wearing high heels. It was very, very funny.

Don doesn't really overdress. He always comes casual. He'll go out to dinner to a fancy place wearing the same clothes he wore in the warehouse. My wife and I were members of the LaGorce Country Club, and we would take them to dinner there and he'd be wearing jeans or something like that with a big key chain full of keys hanging down and he'd be out on the dance floor dancing with these people all dressed up, very proper, and he didn't care. It was great.

I met Don through my wife, who knew him since they were teenagers, I guess. She was a friend of his second wife Johannah. When I married my wife I met him and I immediately knew this guy was an unusual talent, very funny, always entertaining people. He told me one time his ambition really was to be a Vegas lounge comedian because he enjoys entertaining people. When he goes on a cruise and they have a show or whatever in the night club, and when they ask for audience participation he stands up and immediately runs to the stage. Usually you have to beg people to come up from the audience. He goes right up there, wants to be on the stage.

I thought the billboard was great. I used to give him ideas about improving his business and one that I gave him I said, "Don, I notice that these other carpet stores have a fire sale. Why don't you have a pre-fire sale?" He said, "It's a great idea." He took it to his lawyer and insurance company and they said, "Don't you dare."

There was a very popular show off Broadway that ran for years and years, Tony and Tina's Wedding, and it depicted an Irish and Italian wedding. In New York there's a lot of inter-marriage, and historically at those weddings there's usually a lot of fights. Especially years ago. That show was down here a couple of years ago, my daughter knew one of the actors in it and we went down to see it at that theater on Washington Avenue. And we took Don and Donna, it's a hilarious show. There's a wedding and they hire a stripper as part of the show, and she's a gorgeous girl. And I don't know how she sensed Don, but she came over and started stripping in front of him. He loved it. He got up, took off his shirt, he started to take off his pants, he's stripping along with her. It was hilarious, so much so that when we're walking out this one couple said, "You were the best part of the show. Are you in the show?" They thought he was part of it because he did the dance with her and took off his clothes slowly. And the stripper loved it.

One time we walked into a restaurant and Don has a wallet that's very thick because he has a lot of business cards and money in it. It was a very fancy restaurant and he gives the maitre'd his wallet and says, "Make sure we get a good table." The maitre'd looks at the wallet and is shocked. He loves to shock people.

Another time my daughter and her girlfriend were at Aventura Mall and they were looking in the window at a dress shop in the winter. She was like a teenager then, and they're looking in the window and Don sees them and he walks over to them and says, "Hi, how are you? I know why you're looking in the window. I'll bet your father never buys you anything." He pulls out his wallet and gives them each 50 bucks and says, "Go buy yourselves some decent clothes." They thought it was hilarious.

He's a very successful business man. He's very smart, he's one of the smartest guys I've ever met. Even though he doesn't have much formal education he's very smart. I read a lot. Many times I'd bring a subject up and it amazes me about how knowledgeable he was. I remember years ago when nuclear proliferation was a big discussion, he knew a lot about it. And I'd given him books I thought were interesting and he read them all and we'd discuss them. It's something people don't know. They see the showbiz/retailing side of him, but he loves to read books.

Donna is very tolerant of the things he does, and it doesn't faze her at all.

It was a lot of fun to go to New York before Christmas. It's all lit up and Fifth Avenue is gorgeous. And we started going up to appreciate the beauty of New York, and one year my wife and I went up and we stayed at a hotel. When we went back a week or two later I said to Don, "We went to New York before Christmas and we stayed at such and such hotel."

And he said, "I know it. We were there that same weekend. We stayed at the same hotel."

I said, "Really? We should have spoken to each other."

He said, "I knew you were there and I saw you in the lobby but I didn't want to talk with you. I don't want to talk to you in New York. I get enough of you in Miami."

He claims he saw us in the hotel. Donna loved Peggy, there is no way she wouldn't have contacted us if they knew we were there. That's just how Don kids around.

9. CELEBRITY FRIENDS

BUTCH DAVIS

Is there anything you can publish in a book about Don Bailey? It's like the life story of Hugh Hefner. The best parts you can't print.

My exposure to Don is somewhat limited. I first met him in 1984 when I came down to the University of Miami (as part of Jimmy Johnson's staff). One of Don's closest friends was Joe Brodsky, who was on the staff. Don had come to the office to see Joe.

The first time I met him, I thought he was an absolute lunatic. I don't know if it was when I was talking to Don Junior at the time.

I remember seeing him at almost every Hurricane function—the Golden Canes, Dade, Broward and Palm Beach County kickoff functions in August. And he was just hilarious.

I got to know him and when I came back as head coach and Don Junior was back doing broadcasts and color. He had the funniest stories. He's one of those guys we used to absolutely roar with. And there were these legendary Christmas cards Don would send out. The ego of anybody to try to consider pulling that off . . . the muscle pose and flexing his arms.

He loved the UM program a great deal and always was willing to try to help coaches with the nuts and bolts.

The first time I saw the billboard I wondered: Who is this total lunatic? That was before I knew he had anything to do with the program.

Driving up I-95 and seeing it—it's one of the most bizarre marketing concepts. Golly, his son played at Miami?

Whether I saw him outside the locker room after a game or wherever, he reminded me of a cross between Milton Berle and Jackie Gleason. He was always trying to bust somebody.

I remember one time we were trying to get one of meeting rooms carpeted, and Joe Brodsky was trying to work some deal to get Don to donate carpet. There was always some kind of angle or deal. He said, "Whatever you want, whatever color." He absolutely got it done. It's a shame Joe is not here to help write the book.

I saw Don recently, the first time in person since left Miami, at Joe's Stone Crab. Leave it to Don to embarrass me and his wife.

I don't think he has ever met a stranger. He's every man's Rodney Dangerfield, a guy who truly is the one liner and the wit.

RANDY SHANNON

Don is one of the most outgoing and funny guys I've ever met. He's a genuinely funny guy. He'll take a bad situation and make it into a funny situation. He will do it hysterically, anything to break the tension going on.

I met him through Don Junior. He was always involved with Dade County schools, through coach Walt Frazier, coach Joe Brodsky, coaches he's known and people who coached me.

We'd get involved at a party or someone's house, being out. When I was an assistant at UM I went to a Dade Country function and he was the emcee and he was hilarious.

Every time I see him he has hilarious things to talk about. He'll play with his nipples. He's always playing with them, or making sexual comments. He'll make you laugh.

The first time saw the billboard I thought, who is this guy doing this type of things? It was many years ago, probably when I was in high school or maybe going to UM on I-95.

I never knew who the guy was. Then I noticed who he was. Then I got a Christmas card from him wearing bikini underwear.

The picture of him with his three wives? That's him.

Then I've got to send him different things I see on the Internet or I may hear a joke and tell him. He's always a true friend. When there are tough times he is always there to support no matter what.

His mind is always working and keeps working, gets something going.

When you say bright mind, he makes a bad situation great, makes a better situation even better

If you have one dollar, he wants you to have five. If you have five, he wants you to have 10. If you have one house, he wants you to have two. He wants a person to get more and more and better and better. He always supports the underdog.

What drives him? He is always going to be young. He's never going to get old. That's one thing I think drives him. Don Junior worries about him but Don won't let Don Junior worry.

He's unique.

He loves to be part of Miami.

He knows Miami.

He is Miami.

LEE CORSO

I was never as close to Don as I would have liked to have been. I was gone except for a couple of occasions.

He has a great sense of humor. Nobody is funnier than him.

I remember seeing him in the summer with Joe Brodsky and the guys. He was hilarious.

I came back and saw the billboard, and that's hilarious. A spinoff of Burt Reynolds. It's great. He's a marketing genius. Burt was first and Don Bailey was second. A stroke of genius.

The photo of him with his three wives? That's Bailey.

He's a great guy, gave to everybody.

He's a great success story. An American success story.

GARY DUNN

I met Don around UM years ago, just kind of passing through.

"This is Don Bailey Senior," he said.

"Oh, oh yeah?"

I worked out with Don Junior—he's younger than me—when I was with the Steelers and he was playing for the Colts. Through him I was spending time with his dad. I'd go over to his house for parties. I always thought Junior is crazy and Senior is flipping nuts.

We'd be at these parties where all the UM players and coach Art Kehoe and bunch of guys were there. Senior would come in there and be telling all these stories and take over the show. He'd absolutely floor us.

I'd think, What did he just say?

How I got to know him is that I have bar and restaurant in the Keys and he has a place in Key Largo and comes in there all the time. People say, "When is that crazy Don Bailey coming?"

"You mean Junior?

"No, Senior." He's part of the family here.

One time years ago when I was starting to get to know him, they wanted me to say something at the Miami Touchdown Club, tell some stories about FSU.

Senior was going to introduce me. He sits with me and has this piece of paper and is getting information about how long I was with the Steelers, the number of Super Bowls I played in, and about UM.

He starts talking up there about his billboards off of I-95 and people start asking him questions. He's going for 20 minutes and finally says, "I appreciate you all having me," and steps off the podium.

Then he says, "Oh, and Gary Dunn is going to speak a couple of words." That was my introduction.

I grew up in Miami and remember seeing the billboard as a kid. I put the connection together when Don Junior said, "That's my dad on the billboard. My dad,"

I said, "No way."

I thought he was a nut, and there's the nut on the billboard.

He's a smart man, gets people just where he wants them. And he's a good guy.

Another story: Recently I saw this book a doctor wrote about the South Beach Diet. Somebody in the Keys said, "You've got to go to that guy, he's a preventative cardiologist."

So I go there and I'm in Miami Beach laying in a chair, and there's a treadmill around corner and I'm waiting for the guy on it to finish.

They say to the guy, "You think you can go longer?"

The voice says, "If you put a woman in front of me I can go all day."

I said, "Don Bailey Senior, is that you?"

It was. We were busting each other's chops and we could not see each other. What are the odds of that?

FERDIE PACHECO

At the beginning, I never knew Don Bailey. I saw his ad (the billboard). This guy's a nut.

Somebody calls me up and says, "I'll give you $2,000 if you let me rent your apartment during the Super Bowl."

Two thousand bucks. Well, I don't need money, I have all kinds of money but I'm not stupid, either. For $2,000 I'll go sleep any place.

The guy said, "Listen, I've got a friend, Don Bailey, do you know him?" I said, "No, I don't. Yeah, I know him kind of."

He said, "Well his wife . . ."

I said, "I know her."

"They will let you stay in their place for nothing."

I said I don't like to stay any place for nothing, I'd like to pay them something. All I need to do is sleep there during the night. I work all day and all night.

So anyway I stayed there for a month, and of course Don and Johannah were very hospitable. And he loved the idea of being around Ali. He'd come with me to the gym, different places.

"Come on, let's go, I'll take you." So he started coming to fights with us. The things people do around me, they go to fights. He would go every place, He was always very nice, did not bother me at all. He was nice. I just had nothing to say bad or good about him. I told him, "You're cheating on your wife, aren't you? You've got a helluva wife. Pay attention to her, will you? You're gonna lose her. You are gonna lose her."

And we developed a helluva friendship. I watched Dondi grow up and was really nice to him, and I found Don very funny. He is crazier than s—. He is crazy.

I don't know how many wives he had after that. The first was a regular girl who wasn't much. Then was Johannah, who was great. And then he got this next one with big tits who talks a lot. And still married to her. And that was the end of that.

And he is very generous. Extremely generous.

And he's a little on the cheap side.

One story that defines Don Bailey: He calls me up and he's all excited, he's very, very excited. His son, he was a good football player. The (University of Miami) Football Hall of Fame, the yearly thing, Dondi is being honored as the best football player and the leader and this and that.

So Dondi gets up, I'm sitting next to him and Don.

And Dondi gets up and gives a beautiful speech. I didn't think he could do it without breaking down and crying. His speech is about how much his father means to him. It's the kind of speech any father would like to hear. His son is the number one guy on the team then. You are talking about big things here. So Dondi delivers a beautiful speech, quivers a little bit but delivers it. Coaches, everybody was crying. Dondi obviously was very emotional about his father. I wish my son would say something like that to me, would've been great. As it was, I have to speak to his parole officer to see if he wants to say anything.

I said to Don, "Don't screw it up." I know how crazy he is. It's a beautiful moment, don't screw it up.

So he goes up and he says, "I'm moved by my son's speech. I don't deserve all that, but I would like to say one thing. During all that accolades, never once did he mention the rug business. We sell rugs, you know."

(What about his rags to riches story?) It's an American story. If you work a lot at a normal occupation . . . Putting down rugs is nothing, is no science fiction thing. It's just a question about selling something to people. And he did that very well. He knew how to do that. You can not outsell a guy like that, and that's what he did. He's one of these guys that outsold everybody.

Don says I'm the first celebrity he ever met? I don't know about that. What does celebrity mean to people? To me I've always been a normal guy. There's no reason to be anything else. What, because I can paint pictures? Or because I can be a sportscaster? All those things are easy for me.

To get back down to the bottom line is, he's a very cheerful individual who believes that life is just a bowl of cherries. He really does. It's all fun. It's all gonna be fun and everything's going to be OK. And he—I just don't know how to say it—he just thinks everything's going to work out. And it does. So, I love him for what he is, whatever that is.

He is a funny guy, a funny ad libber because he's irreverent. He'll say things that are irreverent.

He says that? I give speeches all the time but not that crazy. But when it comes to a certain point, it's good to have ad lib to your thing.

Do I know about him giving away 14 or 15 cars? No, but that's him. He is a good guy. That I would put in the book. That I believe, because if there's one thing it's his tendency to be kind. He is kind.

He's a guy whose life creeps by before you know it. You going along—this guy, is he around? Oh, he's still got that thing on the . . . and he comes out every year with a nude card. How long has that been, 50, 60 years and he's still doing that? Yeah, he is?

So what I see is a lack of substance. What is he? A fool. That's what he is, a fool. But a nice fool. And he makes money. It truly is sort of perplexing to me.

Geez, that guy's still around? Nothing happen to him?

I like the guy. I like the guy.

He had the incredible lightness of being. That's the key word. He floated over everything. He doesn't live in this world down here, he floats above everything. That's who he is. He's a wafter, and that's him. That's the way I would describe him. That's how I hope they describe him on his tombstone.

One of the popular holiday cards.

Don and Donna with Congressman Kendrick Meek (left)
and President Bill Clinton.

10. EMPLOYEES

AL HINSON

First, some stories:

We were all at a convention, a bunch of carpet people, and just about everybody in that group knew who Don was. We're sitting at a table toward the back, and there were probably 10 tables of 10 people each. The distributor who was putting on the trip had a luncheon, and Don tapped me and said, "I'm going to go change and come back as the nun. I don't want you to point me out when I try to come back in."

So he's gone about 15 to 20 minutes, and he sneaks back in and sits at the table and he's in the nun's outfit.

So the guy is up there speaking or talking to the group, and I don't know if he notices Don come in or not but all of a sudden the nun catches his eye. And he says something like, "And by the way everybody, I want you to know in our presence today we have one of the sisters from the nearest parish," or whatever. The guy played right in it.

Don stood up and started talking and got so embarrassed he started laughing at himself. He sat back down and everybody was going hysterical and he took off. It was just one of those moments where you had to be there. It was unbelievable.

We were also on a trip one time, this might have been Switzerland or Italy. They're off doing a conga line and at the end of the line here's Don and he's naked and he's got these roses he'd picked up from somewhere between his legs up his butt coming out the back. And he's the last one on the conga line. Of course that brought the house down.

We were also having dinner one night at this bar out in the middle of nowhere, out in farm pasture, and Dick Bartlett gets an idea as we're pulling up to the barn house. There are pens and sheep in them.

Well, Bartlett has a few drinks and has the idea that we're going to go out and catch one of these sheep and bring it back in to the party. He's out there and says, "I'm going to get one and bring it back for Don Senior."

He's out there and he tries to catch one of these sheep and he's half in the bag already, and he slips and falls flat out in the mud. Covered in mud. Finally he decides he's not going to be able to get one, and he comes back in and he's drenched in mud and we're explaining we were trying to catch a sheep for Don Senior and it never happened. He's full of mud head to toe.

I was probably 8 or 9 years old when I met Don and we lived a block away from each other. So I was just at the age where I was probably allowed to leave my block and go play with the neighborhood kids. I had some kids that lived directly behind me that we played with.

What happened was, the neighborhood kids would come and play. Well, some of the kids were coming from two blocks away. Everybody had their bicycles and started riding around.

We used to play close to my house when I was 7 or 8 years old. I had to be within shouting distance because when my mom called my name I better be answering back and be getting home. If I was out of shouting distance, I was in trouble.

We were always playing these pickup games and kids from the other blocks are coming down. So finally they said there's a better place to play to go play football. It was in front of Don's house. So we all go down the street and start playing there.

Don had the best house, best front yard, and we played football in the front yard. And in the back they had a huge tree with a tree fort in it. That was only a dream; you never realized you'd ever be in a real tree fort.

So that was it. That became the playground for the next two, three, four years. We were always there. I probably was playing with Don Junior and met his mom first, being at the house. She was always out there making sure that we weren't picking on anybody. And inevitably by the end of the day with a bunch of kids playing, somebody was crying for one reason or the other.

A couple of years later, maybe I was about 10 or 11. I'm three years older than Don Junior, so he was smaller than us. Some were his age, some were a little older. And once in awhile she asked me to watch the kids while she ran to the store and said don't leave until she came home. So I'd kind of watch them and we were just in the back yard playing in the tree fort. It started from there.

I know Don had just left Harry Rich and went into business. I didn't know this exactly. It wasn't his own company yet, it was Expressway Carpet with two or three other people. I remember going to that business at that location on a Saturday or something and I'd go with Don Junior and we'd go over there, maybe sweep the warehouse and clean up.

They moved from the neighborhood when I was 12 years old, moved to San Souci, rented a house while they were having a house built. In that transition as well, he had opened his own business, Don Bailey Carpet. That was in August of '71.

In October he called me because I didn't see him as much because they had moved away, and at 12 years old I wouldn't ride my bike there. It was too far for me to go, unless they came and got me to go bowling or to a football game.

I didn't see Don Junior as much, then his dad called and said he opened this store on 98th Street, and it was close enough to ride my bike to. So I was able to come home from school and go there and work after school.

I'd get there at 3:30 and work there until 5:30 or 6 o'clock and try to work as much on a Saturday. I had just turned 13 and was going to Horace Mann Junior High. I would walk to school and back, it was five blocks from my house. Then I would ride my bike over there.

They had one guy at the warehouse that worked part-time also, and I kind of helped him do whatever he wanted when he needed help. There was no machinery, no forklift, no hoisters. Everything was done by hand. Pull a roll of carpet down, put it on the dollies, get it in the warehouse, roll it out, cut it. Roll it back up and try to put it back on a pile.

We were probably there two years without any forklift. Finally the business grew enough where he could afford to buy a forklift.

The only other thing I was doing back then was delivering newspapers, and I stopped doing that because after school I was there (at the warehouse) and felt I could make more money there than delivering the newspapers.

That was the start of it and it's 40 years ago this year.

My title is vice president and part owner. There's myself, Don Junior and I believe Don Senior still owns a part of it, but I believe his share is in Brett's name. So there's three of us still as owners of Don Bailey's.

And that was given to me for being in the business I guess for so long he felt that . . . He had brought Don Junior in and had actually given all of the kids part of the business. They all did work here at one time or another but just felt it wasn't their cup of tea. Bobby was here for awhile as part owner, as well as Jeannie Bailey. For whatever reason, not being able to get along with maybe dad or maybe Junior or whatever, the situation was just felt that it was better for the family for them not to work together.

And even today with Don Junior, Don Senior and myself, none of us really work under the same roof together. For whatever reason, it just works out better that way. Everybody has their own roles. Right now we do our own thing and that's what makes the company work. We meet once a week as a group, including my wife, who is also comptroller of the company. She's in on that and we basically have what we call the owners' meeting to discuss what's going on, what's coming up and that sort of thing.

I have no complaints or regrets. I've been offered probably a dozen or two dozen jobs in my lifetime, and I've just told people there's nothing else that I'd rather do than where I'm at. And to me I felt too loyal even to come to them and say I want to go to something else. It just never entered my mind. I don't know why, I just didn't feel that way.

Maybe because even my mom, a single parent, worked for the same company for 30 or 35 years herself. And I just maybe as growing up said to myself, "You get a job, you're supposed to keep it. Don't go looking for another job, don't take another job. You've got a job." And I didn't know any better, I guess. I don't know. They gave me the opportunity to have a job and I did the best I could at it.

I raised two kids, I've been through a few wives. And I don't know if that's because of the surroundings around me. And I can't blame it on anybody but whatever happened in my life is mine. Other than kidding around.

And I always tell people when they say, "You've been there so long, why have you been there so long?" I just tell them I really believe I'm an illegitimate son of Don Senior anyway. He just doesn't want to tell me because then he's got to put me in the will for a full amount instead of giving me what he wants.

That's my standing joke when anybody asks me why I've been around Don so long.

The work ethic here has been there from Day One. When I came and worked after school two hours, there was no sitting down. There was always something to do. I'd come in and have a list of things to make sure this was done, that was done. The trash was out, the floor was vacuumed, the bathrooms were clean, the warehouse was swept.

If I was able to get to the bottom of that list on a daily basis, I would have been lucky. There was never any time, and there again that was just the way I was taught to be doing something. If you're at work you're supposed to be working. And that was just the ethic of it and how I was raised with it.

And I'll go back to my mom again, she was the same way. She went to work, she was a hard worker, she devoted her life to a company and never thought about doing anything else. She went up as high in that company as she could go. And from then on, you work as hard as you can as long as you can.

You talk work ethic, you talk about working for what you want, and if you work hard and make things happen, there are rewards. And I've been rewarded.

My life at this point has been fulfilled. I've raised two kids, I've had wonderful times, wonderful memories. And I can't even go back and say there's something else I would want to do again. I have no regrets whatsoever.

It's been fun and it seems to be more fun as time goes on. I think Don Senior, there was a lot of pressure on him in his younger days, whether I realized it or not.

I mean, I probably understand them a little more now only because I'm older and I understand about business and expenses and paying the bills and paying the people who are working for you and realizing all that. He had not only his own family to take care of, the company was a family as well. And if there were 10, 20, 30 or 40 employees, you know, every morning they woke up and it was Don Bailey who was making sure their family was being taken care of.

He's always been loyal to me and I've always tried to be loyal to any of the employees that I'm in contact with or have a direct relationship with. If there's anything that I can do that I see that I can help out with, I've always tried to help them because he's always done that. I've seen him help them either by giving them a job or by helping them when they needed help because he felt it was the right thing to do. I'd have to say I've learned that from him as well. If you can help someone to the best of your ability, help them.

He shows up every day. If he's in town he's at work. And we try to encourage him: Please go. He has a place in the Keys, he has a place in Vermont. Go and enjoy that. And he has and he'll admit that he has taken time to go out and enjoy life a little bit, and go on these cruises.

I think he feels that he's able to do that and knows that he can go and the people here—myself, Don Junior, Deborah—can keep the company running and he doesn't have to worry about it. And over the years he has tried basically to delegate a lot of things that he does, just to make it easier on him.

That's another thing we always said: If you surround yourself with good people, it makes your life and your business a lot easier. Those are things he's tried to teach and instill in us. And it doesn't always work out that way, where he's trying to help somebody he knows by bringing them in here and giving them a job, and whether it was the right thing to do is questionable. But in his heart he felt he was doing the right thing.

We've had issues and hard feelings about certain people that didn't work out for whatever reason, but you've also got to make a business decision at the end.

I feel I'm letting the company down if I'm not here working. Why? I don't know. I'm sure that's his feeling too. If he's in town he feels he needs to be here and be productive in the business, and I'm that way too.

And even with my wife Deborah, she's in the same mode of we eat, sleep and breathe the job. And probably—I'm not going to say that was a factor in other relationships but—the understanding wasn't there. If you weren't here working this job, if Deborah wasn't here working she probably wouldn't understand. You know, getting up at 6 o'clock, 5:30 in the morning to get to work and getting home at 8 or 9 o'clock. People don't understand that, unless you're here living it.

I never questioned if I had to do something early or late as far as the job, and I probably put the job, the business, more in front than family. Not trying to hurt anybody's feeling. That's got to work for everything else to run smoothly. You've got to make sure that business is running to make the life run. And some people just didn't understand that. It probably played into relationships because they didn't understand.

Not that I could have done anything differently, and I probably could have. But I couldn't see why they didn't understand. I couldn't get that point across to where they did understand.

And look at how understanding Donna is, because she's been through it all with the business and everything else throughout his life. And she understands the whole picture. You've got to give a little to get a lot a lot of times. There's got to be give and take.

The work ethic, and his competitiveness: That goes back many years, too, because when I was growing up we would go one afternoon from 3 o'clock to 6 o'clock to play racquetball. It was Dick Bartlett and Don, always a group of about four or five people, mostly their friends. I got old enough where I would go and play.

The competitiveness was always there, and then we started playing tennis and we did go out of town one time. We were playing tennis and I was probably in my teens and I had a little bit of a step on him. And if you had a step on him active-wise, he was going to try to out-talk you and try to beat you. Get into your head if he couldn't beat you physically. He was going to try to beat you mentally, try to talk you out of your game.

We were playing tennis up in North Carolina. They had taken me on vacation and I probably was 16 or 17 years old, and he goes to take a swing at a ball and he barely got to it or I don't think he got to it and he brings the racquet up and hits himself in the eye. Cuts a gash open in his eye.

So that was the end of that. He asks me and I say, "It's bleeding, it's pretty bad. You probably should get stitches."

So we're walking back to the room or he's going to go back to the hotel and there's about a two-foot wall as we're walking through this big field from where the tennis courts were to the hotel. And I'm not realizing he's not seeing it because he's holding his eye.

So I jump over the wall, and of course he trips over it. So to add insult to injury, I'm trying not to laugh because he's trying to walk and act like he's got a one-inch gash his eye, and now he just put a big gash on his shin. And it was like one comedy after another. I'm trying not to laugh and he's trying to act like nothing's wrong cause of the competitive edge.

No big deal, no big deal.

We didn't go to the hospital. I think he went in and tried to put a butterfly on something that. He should have gotten stitches. But he wasn't going to the hospital, it wasn't that big a deal. He had a little injury and was going to take care of it himself.

He played active tennis for 20 years at least. And Donna got him playing even more, got him away from the racquetball.

You're going to have to put on the back of the book one his notes about something. It's going to have to be one of his hand-written notes because everybody has gotten notes.

The best one as far as a laugh was to Don Junior, I want to say during his first year of college. He had a brand new El Camino. So they're all out drinking one time, the teammates, and they're getting ready to go home.

I guess Don Junior felt he was in no position to drive, so somebody else took the car keys. Two or three guys get in the back of the El Camino. If you're familiar with an El Camino, it was like a car with an open back, like a pickup truck.

So he's in the back of the El Camino with a couple other football players on their way home. Somebody else is driving the car and they hit a parked car. Well, Don Bailey Junior comes over the top of the hood onto the pavement.

The next he remembers he's waking up in Doctors Hospital, full of road rash, wondering what's going on. They call his dad, and his dad comes down.

"Well what happened? Who was driving?"

And the next day Don Junior got a note that turned into a letter.

He said, "If anybody wants to drive your car, hand them this note."

And Don Junior had to carry it with him in his wallet. If anybody was caught driving that car, it was going to be taken away from him.

Just hand them this note and they'll say, "Never mind."

My first memory of the billboard? Well, we saw the Burt Reynolds centerfold that came out in Cosmopolitan. It was a big to do, it was on the news, it was here.

I don't know if we had two stores yet or one, but I know he put the billboard on the side of the building and from there on it was history. It was nothing but an attention getter for anybody who saw it and came to the store. He even had an Excalibur back then, I want to say in '75, that he had that billboard on the back of that car, almost like a cab-type situation.

I used to get to drive the Excalibur only because Don Senior would go out of town and he would take my car because he didn't want to take the Excalibur out of town if he was going up to Vero Beach or something.

He just didn't want to put all those miles on it. I'd let him use my car. I'd say, "Sure, you can use my car any time you want, I'll gladly change cars and drive the Excalibur." Because whenever I had the Excalibur we were around town cruising with the boys. I mean, that was like a showstopper in itself, and then with the billboard on the back it was doubly an attention getter.

The billboard has definitely brought ranges (of emotions) from everybody. There was a church over by 148th Street that one of the members of the church came into the store to buy carpet for himself and said, "You know I'm on the board of such and such a church and were talking about changing carpet, and I mentioned that I come over here and they wouldn't use you because you've got that sign out there on that wall."

That's probably about the only time I've heard anybody say anything that they didn't come to Don Bailey because that sign was on the wall. We've probably done more churches in Dade, Broward and Palm Beach counties than any carpet store in existence.

She said, "I'm gonna buy carpet from you but they won't do it as a congregation. They don't like that sign you've got out there on the wall, they just won't do it. And I tried to tell them there's nothing going on here. But they just won't give in."

Just in closing, I've always felt that I've been part of the family. It's not like I work here, it's part of my life. My business, my family. And that's how I've always been treated. I was brought up as a single parent family with my mom.

I've know the Baileys since I was 8 or 9 years old, and since that time on I've always had a dad. That's why I'm still here and why I'll always be here. I've never questioned anything they've asked me to do. I've just done it. And if I've needed anything, they've done it for me. That's been the way of Don Bailey Senior, to do whatever he can do for those that needed to be done for.

DEBBIE HINSON

I played basketball for the University of Miami and Don Junior played football, and we were got to know each other through that. And Don Junior ended up marrying a roommate of mine during the time I was there. So we kind of all hung out together there.

And after Hurricane Andrew hit in 1992, the carpet company went skyrocketing with a lot of people obviously needing flooring and there was a big influx of business. And Don Junior called me up one day and said he was in need of somebody to run his office. They didn't really have a good handle on the office and were way too busy.

I had an interview and was hired 19 years ago. I previously had worked for the accountant for Don Bailey Carpet. He had a Panama Jack distributorship, so I was running that for him and I was working temporarily, and Don called and it worked out perfectly.

I ended up marrying Al, who is a partner. He's been here from Day One with Don Senior, I had even known Al, knowing Don. Wherever Don had a party or wherever we went out as a big group, Al was always around because Don Junior and Al where childhood friends and remained friends and are now business partners.

Then I came into the business. I was single and he happened to be single and it worked out from there.

The loyalty . . . I'm basically that way, I was raised that way. Wherever you are or whatever you're doing you need to give it your 100 percent. If you're name's associated with it make everybody associated with it proud. The loyalty is definitely there.

At times I say I'm comptroller. I'm actually head of operations, director of operations.

What's it like working for Don Senior? I've learned so much from him. He's had a million years in the business. He always says, "Well, when I was manager of operations, this is what my boss always told me."

The other thing that sticks in my head, he always taught that there are two sides to every story. You can't just take the one side. You've got to hear all sides of every story and then make your determination.

He's great. Right now Senior is a lot of fun to be with and learn from him. Don Junior has always said, "When—and we hope it's never but—when something does happen to my father and he's no longer with us I need to have a replacement. And there's only one person in this company that could ever replace him and it's you, Deborah."

I'm like, wow.

He said, "What I mean is that whole operational thing."

I said, "Well, good, I thought you were talking about laying naked on the side of the building, and I don't know if that's good for business or not."

What I've tried to do in all my years here is suck all of the knowledge out of his head that I could. Everything he's learned, all of his experiences. Everything about why this, how this, how did you know to buy your buildings that you own? And he instills a lot of that now.

Very interesting, very awesome.

He's great, very fair, his heart is so good. When he goes on a cruise he brings the girls in the office back a little trinket of something just to say, "On my cruise, when I was relaxing, I was thinking about you guys." And that goes such a long way. He's been such a giving person his whole life.

Just fairly recently, like within a year, I've taken over the warehouse and the warehouse boys, or men. That has always been Don Senior's little entourage, and just learning his ways and how he treats them. A unique group. They're not educated scholars, but they're such an important part and he lets them know. So I try to learn from him how to treat people in regards to your business, yet at the same time applying discipline and making sure that they understand what needs to be done.

Don Senior has been a great leader and still is.

When we have a management meeting, it's Don Junior, Al and Senior and myself, and something will come up and he'll tell a story and Junior and Al are crying they're laughing so hard. There's so much history with Don Senior, where his brother will walk in the door, or this person walks in and he just has so much history that every day is such a unique day.

The one thing you don't want to do, when he's hyping out and he's on a roll, you do not want to be the one who's stopping him from accomplishing what he wants to accomplish. He's very strong headed in that regards too. You work with him. "Yeah, good idea. Let's go, let's get it done and let it flow."

He's a great example. I hope that at 78 I'm working here just as hard as he is.

Don has a house in the Keys and so do Al and I, and so we try to get together the four us with Donna. Company gatherings, maybe twice a year, definitely a Christmas party.

And if company quarterly goals are reached we do something company-wide. Last year we went bowling and had a competition. Teams were selected. It had to have been one of our most fun nights, and we incorporated a sales meeting with that. I think the bowling was the topic of conversation the whole next week. They're funny, good times, half of it due to Don Senior being Don Senior.

I always say I don't want to work, but that's not going to happen unless I win that lovely Powerball. I've always had the energy and work ethic. My goal in life . . . I got an accounting degree from the University of Miami. That wasn't what I wanted to do. I wanted to be a high up somewhere and run a business.

When I left school I worked for a bank and then a company that gave hundreds of millions in financial aid and had to keep track. I was moving up but it got stagnant, it was OK. And then I came into Don Bailey's, just the closeness of Don and Al and Senior.

It just grew. This is it. The only other job I ever wanted was probably to take the place of Obama. I wish I had been hired as President. I can balance the budget. I don't know why that's so hard. I've never really thought of going elsewhere. It's family.

My first reaction to the billboard? Oh, my God. That's what I said.

And that was when I was in college, and then I just never thought about it. Every year we'd get in the dorm, and when the full year started we always went to Don's dad to get new carpet for our dorm.

So we pulled up and sure enough, there's the billboard. I go, "Oh, my God, Don, aren't you embarrassed? That's your dad."

And he's like, "No, that's kind of cool, that's really cool."

It never really came up more. Whenever you saw Don Bailey, you thought of the son. I never thought much of it until I got hired. And even when Don called me I never thought about the billboard—until my dad was coming down to visit. And I thought, "Ohhhhh, nooooo! Oh, no! How and I going to explain this? "

We had a going away party and my dad was down. This was like eight years ago or so, and my dad was invited to this dinner, a going away party for one of the employees that was retiring, and dad was down visiting me.

Don Senior got up and said, "Hi, I want to say that I am a lesbian." He gave that story. Well, my dad is there, and I think, "Ohhhhh, I'm going to get this speech from my dad and he is going to tell me, 'You've got to come home. I mean, this isn't the right thing for you.'"

And I come to find out, it was never really brought up after the dinner. But Don went on his whole spiel about being a lesbian and how his brother was his first sex partner and all this stuff. When the dinner was over and we go home it was never brought up. And this was in March or April. And I go home for Christmas to Ohio and my step mother is telling me, "You know, your father went to the country club and tells everybody the story, tells everybody that he thinks he's a lesbian just like what Don said."

So apparently my father loved the story and started using it. And here I was worried. "Oh, my God, he's going to give me this talk. Is this really what you want?" It was so funny.

We always looked at Don Junior at school like, what? I came from strict Catholic background. And then my family members come down and, what? And then you tell the story. And Senior told me the story of how it all started, so when people hear that, then they understand.

So I go, "Well Don, why does your dad like to be nude?" And he says, "Oh, he's not really nude there. He's got shorts on, the painter just painted it."

He always implemented fun into every day that he had to go to work. If I'm in a business meeting and it's, "Don Bailey? Isn't that the . . . ?"

"Yes, yes, you can stop there. Yes it is, yes, that's the naked carpet man."

"My God, you work for him? Is he still alive? Is that Al on the board.?

"Yeah, that's Al, that's my husband."

People must ask all the time if that's Al on the board.

It started out like, "Oh, my gosh, I can't let anybody know." And now I see how they came into it. It's not a real big deal.

We send out thank you cards and on the front of the cards there's Don's pose. And you send that to a church? Well, a church can certainly buy from us, right? What's the problem? It's not any disrespect to God or anything. It's OK. The Bible is full of sexuality, if people want to make it sexuality.

It's always been fun. He always has a joke. And as he's gotten older his jokes are about his old age, you know. The farting he does, or whatever older people do.

The one that always stands in my mind is the one where he's standing naked like a remnant, like a piece of carpet.

He knows what I go through in running the operation and how he's so respected, and the one lady that ran the office and the books and all for when he worked for Harry Rich. He'd been in contact with her his whole life, because she's passed away now. And he always sent her a birthday card because she made such an impact.

So he's always telling me these personal experiences, so that's who you need to be for some of the warehouse guys or some of the sales people.

If he finds somebody is stealing carpet, Don always gets real quiet, because he stole carpet, or he stole when he started out. He'll go into the story, "Well, when I was a truck driver for Harry Rich, I told a guy, 'Give me that one over here.'" Stories about when he was growing up, and he and Jimmy and all sleeping in one bedroom and coming down in the station wagon (from Georgia). He tells me about Harry Rich, and his stories about his divorces are pretty funny also.

And if we go to a business meeting he'll introduce me as his bitch. You just never know what's coming up. And when Don Junior wants him on his best behavior, he'll let him know. "Hush, not here." Something along those lines. There's a million stories.

Al was an only child and didn't really have his dad around. His mom is who raised him and Al got to be friends with Don Junior, and then Don Junior's mother would call Al to come over and babysit Don Junior and Bobby because Al is like four years older than Junior. They became really close friends. When Al was 13, they were over at the house one night and horsing around and Don Senior said, "Why don't you just start coming after school on you bike and sweep the floors or do something. Help me out, OK?" Thirty-five years later, Al has had no other job but this one.

RICHARD FAISON

I've worked for 15 years for Don, mostly at this warehouse on 83rd Street. He brought me in through a friend of mine. I work at the warehouse and drive a truck. He told me that's how he started.

Being around him and seeing what a wonderful person I think he is, it was truly meant for him to be blessed that way. Even though he worked hard to get where he's at, I see the way he worked and hope that one day I can be that kind of person—work hard and be able to successful like him. I think it's real good that he's in the position he's in.

It's very motivational for young people the way he tells how hard he worked and how he came along. It's real good.

He's the best. The best. A father.

Some times I get emotional when people ask me about him because he's been so good to me. I've never met anybody like him. And I mean that from my heart.

If you work hard for him, he treats you just like a son, for real. Like I say, I get emotional because he is genuine. Like a father I never had for real. He really is.

I'm from Georgia, a little small place called Abbeville, which has one red light. I came here in 1987 when I was 21.

I learned to work hard, and if you work hard it pays off. You get rewarded for being honest. He taught me to be honest. I learned to be kind to people. Do unto others as you want them . . . I learned that.

Being around him you understand that more. The way he's been good to me, and the way it makes me feel, I think to myself that's the way I want to make others feel.

I learned to be determined and make things right. If you can help it, if you can be a part of it, be determined to make it right. And work hard, that's the main thing.

Other job offers have come along a few times in 15 years, but Don Senior . . . I can't express it enough. He's such a good person that you think in your mind that you can't find another good boss.

It's like a blessing to me that he's so good. Why would you look somewhere else? I guess it's like a good relationship. If you're with someone good, make it happen.

He always tries to make things fun. Always. Some times I come to work and sit at my desk and he gets on the phone and I'm sitting next to him and he just gets to joking with whoever is on the phone, and I just laugh, man. He's good, making your day better. Real good.

He's told me so many good jokes, I just go home and tell my family about them. That's his second thing, keeping people laughing. I know that's the way he lives. He works hard and in order to make people feel good when things aren't going good. He's good at it.

He does more than have office parties. He gives cars to the warehouse guys when you work hard. And helps you get a house. He made a way for me to get a home. That's what I'm so proud of. That's why I say what I say.

Gave a car, did not ask for a penny. He may have given me about five cars since I've been here. About the nicest thing—he bought himself a brand new truck and gave me his pickup truck.

And one thing I really get emotional about: One time I was looking for an apartment and I could have stayed with my sisters and brothers but he thought I had nowhere to stay, and he had a two-story house and had a room down below and offered me that room to stay in until I found myself a place to stay.

I was taking the bus coming to work. At first I lived right down the street from his store and I walked to work. When I went to this store on 83rd Street, that's about 15 to 20 minutes away. And he got me a car. An Oldsmobile Delta 88.

I had a father and I loved my father dearly. My father passed and Don took over as my father.

He's been the role, he does the things a father would do for a son and really more because he doesn't have to.

I think the reason he's so close to the warehouse is because that's where he started out working. He knows about hard working in the warehouse. He's the best.

A funny thing to me, he was telling me about he and his wife. His wife saw someone jumping over the wall one day and his wife wasn't working and she called the police. And the police came and about a week later someone else jumped over the wall and she called the police again. He said, "All right, I'm tired of this. It's time for you to stop doing this policeman watch and time to get you a real job."

Whatever I need, when I go to him he never says no.

I hadn't seen the billboard until I came to work here. The first thing I thought was comedy. When I was interviewed for the job he would tell you stories and make you laugh. So when I saw that billboard I thought that's another one of his jokes. Just being himself.

(Anything else?) Just that I love the man.

LESHAN KELLY

I got my job with Don through my fourth grade teacher at Palmetto Elementary, Mrs. Comendeiro. She was like a mom to me when I was growing up.

I was in a foster home and was still in high school and needed a job. And she had me talk to Don Junior, who played football at Miami with her husband, Juan. I met Don Senior in 1998.

One time I called Mrs. Comendeiro and asked her if she could help me out any way. I graduated in June in 1999, and the foster home put me out in '99. I didn't know where I was going to go. When I going to court Don Senior went to court with me, took me back to foster home and took me to a place he had, like a room. Something like a father would do.

Mainly I do warehousing, customer service, answer the phone, maintaining the warehouse, or if salesmen need help.

I see Don on a regular basis. He has been like a father figure to me, as well as a good employer. The whole family has. I'm very blessed and grateful.

He's definitely a good guy, He bought me my first car and my first drum set. I play in a band and I still have it.

He paid for my vacation to the Bahamas several times. If my car breaks down, he makes sure it's running.

Before I went to work here I had seen the billboard but it never really caught my attention as a kid, not until I started working for him. I lived in North Miami and I remember seeing it. While driving on I-95 and seeing it on a pink building. I didn't know Mrs. Comendeiro knew him.

When I went to work, the first thing I thought was, "Wow." I never thought about being there. It was just weird.

He's a funny guy, now that I know him I can see the mindset behind the billboard, his sense of humor.

He's definitely a hard-working man. He shows up every day. When I first started he was moving carpet around even though he's older man. He's always dedicated to the people in the store. Nothing is too big or small for him. He's about business first and foremost and expects you to do your job and be responsible. But he has a sense of humor.

He never misses a beat. He has a smart memory, writes everything down, a thousand notes in his pocket. You don't see a lot people with details like that.

He told me his story. I think he's very smart. Knowing Don, I can see him doing that. He still remains down to earth no matter how much money you have. I think he'd be the same whether he had money or not. You never know he's Don Bailey unless you know him.

He helps out others and doesn't put himself above anybody. He's like a fatherly mentor, how to do the right thing, be responsible when you come to work and be professional. This was my first job ever.

He really appreciates hard work, when do your job and be an honest person. When you call him he is always there.

I really appreciate him and thank him a lot. It's one great family to me.

Don with Dick Bartlett and Don Junior.

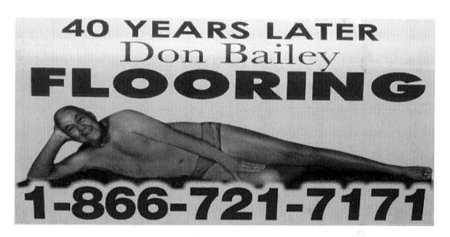

40 years later.